ALL YOU
EVER WANTED

ALL YOU
EVER WANTED

a devotional and small group study on the fruit of the spirit

DR. WIN GREEN

TATE PUBLISHING & *Enterprises*

All You Ever Wanted
Copyright © 2008 by Dr. Win Green. All rights reserved.

The opinions expressed by the author are not necessarily those of Tate Publishing, LLC.

Published by Tate Publishing & Enterprises, LLC
127 E. Trade Center Terrace | Mustang, Oklahoma 73064 USA
1.888.361.9473 | www.tatepublishing.com

Tate Publishing is committed to excellence in the publishing industry. The company reflects the philosophy established by the founders, based on Psalm 68:11,
"The Lord gave the word and great was the company of those who published it."

Book design copyright © 2008 by Tate Publishing, LLC. All rights reserved.
Interior design by Joey Garrett

Published in the United States of America

ISBN: 978-1-60604-531-2
1. Biblical Study-Devotional
3. Exegesis-History
8.06.11

FOR
My Bride Stephanie!
Je t'aime de tout mon coeur!

ACKNOWLEDGEMENTS:

Thanks and praise go to those who helped bring this book to life.

First and foremost to my wife Stephanie, who gave her wholehearted support and love for this project. I can hardly think without talking, and Stephanie is the one with whom I love talking the most. All the ideas for this book generated from our ongoing conversation. You are my great love!

Everglades Community Church in Pembroke Pines, Florida and The Nassau Christian Center in Princeton, New Jersey both supported me as I worked out ideas from their pulpits. Both congregations provided the backdrop for much of what is written in these pages.

My heartfelt thanks go to Maxie Dunnam and Ellsworth Kalas, both presidents of the great Asbury

Theological Seminary in Wilmore, Kentucky. These two giants inspired and encouraged me to serve God as a pastor, and to write my thoughts and experiences on paper. Both gave their precious time to read rough drafts of this book and to offer their insights. I treasure them both.

Sincere gratitude goes to professors Luke Powery and Stacey Johnson of Princeton Thological Seiminary. They read through the rough drafts of this book and cheered me on to the finish line. Thanks for your friendship!

I am grateful to Congressman Todd Platts, who, in the middle of an incredibly busy schedule, somehow managed to read through the manuscript of this book and offer his support! You are a true public servant, and a friend.

Dean Alison Boden of Princeton University offered her support after reading the manuscript. I am grateful for your kindness and graciousness.

Suzanne Orris, a dear friend and a perceptive critic, poured over these pages in the hope that they would enourage others. You've been a wonderful source of wisdom.

I benefited from many generous editors who took their precious time to read my manuscript and offer their counsel. This book is infinitely better because of their insights: Kat & Spencer Silverglate, Kyle Kaker, Rev. Kevin Brubaker, Rev. Storm Nicole Hutchenson; Meg & John Hauge, and Jay Gayoso, Michael Montgomery, and Alan Kingston.

My gratitude is extended to the Florida Annual

Conference of the United Methodist Church and Bishop Timothy Whitaker for their ongoing support and affirmation of my calling.

And thanks to my new friends at Tate Publishing: Wayne Lin my editor, Melanie Hughes my graphic artist, and Trinity Tate who chose to take a chance on publishing this book.

And special thanks to my parents Ted and Karon Green and family, who weren't always able to understand my life's calling, but who gave me everything they had to give. I love you.

TABLE OF CONTENTS

HOW TO USE
THIS BOOK

This book is designed for two complementary purposes. It is first a devotional intended to inspire and edify individuals who want to grow deeper in their relationship with Jesus Christ. Each of the first nine chapters focuses on one of the nine spiritual fruit St. Paul lists in his letter to the Galatians.

> "But the fruit of the Spirit is love, joy, peace, patience, kindness, goodness, faithfulness, gentleness, self-control ... "
>
> Galatians 5:22–23

These nine fruit are the attributes grown from a relationship with Jesus Christ. As a devotional I suggest this book be read at the pace of one chapter a week, or one chapter a day. After finishing each chapter it is best to give yourself some time to reflect on what God might be saying to you through your reading, before you begin the next chapter. Again, this book's first purpose is to help you grow spiritually by guiding you through a personal reflection on each of the nine fruit of the spirit.

The book's second purpose is to facilite a small group study and discussion. It is hoped that Sunday School classes, small growth groups, and home Bible studies will use this book collectively as a ten week study. Every chapter concludes with an outline for group discussion. Ideally, each participant will have read the preceeding chapter before their group's weekly meeting. A facilitator will then lead the group through the questions at chapter's end while keeping one eye on the clock. These questions are specifically designed to stimulate discussion. This study doesn't strive to articulate right and wrong answers. Instead, it is a study intended to help you experience for yourself (and as a group) each of the nine fruit of God's Spirit.

I hope and pray that this book will bless you!

INTRODUCTION:

Sweet is the promise of ripening fruit. But there is an even sweeter promise planted in the pages of scripture. It is this ... that when the Spirit of God plants itself in your heart it will yield NINE different kinds of spiritual fruit. Saint Paul expressed this heavenly promise when he wrote:

> "But the fruit of the Spirit is love, joy, peace, patience, kindness, goodness, faithfulness, gentleness, self-control; against such there is no law."
>
> *Galatians 5:22–23*

Imagine, nine different fruit from only one seed! It defies the logic of our earth-bound experience, whose science presumes one fruit per corn.

But God can be counted on to be more generous than our earth-bound presumptions. He is the creative genius that finds it impossible to contain His extravagant nature. In the Bible we read of how God turns the morning dew to bread, water to wine, and five loaves with two fish into a feast for thousands. It's just too confining for God to limit His divine seed to but one kind of fruit. And so we have nine, the first of which is love.

The pages that follow are the harvest I've gleaned of each of God's spiritual fruit. It is by no means comprehensive. It is only a taste, which I trust is enough, for the scripture promises:

"O taste and see that the Lord is good!"

Psalm 34:8

CHAPTER ONE: LOVE

You Don't Have To Like 'Em to Love 'Em

I received a crushing letter from a dear friend who described in painful detail how alcohol ruined his wife's life and destroyed their marriage. When his wife didn't drink, she slept. And on the rare occasion when she was neither drunk nor asleep, she fought with family members. This woman was brilliant—with a doctorate in public health and an MBA in finance! As a young woman, she was beautiful and vivacious, and my friend fell for her at first sight. But alcohol robbed her of everything and gutted their marriage. Their family life had disintegrated into chaos, the house was a wreck, and their neighbors were turned off. Most of all, her husband's heart was broken. His agonized letter ended with the presumption that the only obvious end to the devastation of alcoholism in their marriage was his wife's death, for she refused treatment of any kind. His letter was prophetic. Two years later, she literally drank herself to death. Her husband stayed in their marriage to the very end, and he paid a heavy emotional price, but he believed that in this instance it was the best thing to do for everyone involved.

I begin with a simple question: What do you do when you dislike, if not hate, someone you're supposed to love? It may be an intrusive mother-in-law, a rebellious child, or your very own husband or wife. Remember the old expression "familiarity breeds contempt." It's true. Everyone is flawed, so you can find something to dislike about anyone, especially those with whom you're close. No one looks good under a microscope. The closer you get to someone the more likely you are to find something to dislike. The great Russian novelist Fyodor Dostoevsky expressed it well when he wrote, "One can love one's neighbor in the abstract or even at a distance. But at close quarters, it's almost impossible!"

My own first year of marriage is an example of what I'm describing. In our first year together, Stephanie and I discovered things we didn't like about the other. Stephanie detested my love for sports television—especially Monday Night Football. I also hurt her with my lack of sensitivity and empathy, especially when she was sick in bed and I didn't bother to look in on her and make a fuss. And she despaired that I didn't enjoy pillow talk—deep and searching conversation late into the night before falling asleep. I was a disappointing husband. After one particularly bitter and tearful argument, Stephanie shoved her hands on her hips, leaned forward, and with narrowing eyes said, "You know, if we were still dating right now, I'd break up with you." But then she collapsed into tears and cried, "But I can't—We're married!"

Crushed and hurt, at that moment Stephanie hated me. But we worked it out, not by following our instincts or impulses or any of today's popular psycho-babble that parades itself as wisdom. Instead, we followed an ancient prescription for marriage, "Submit yourselves one to another out of reverence for Christ!" (Ephesians 5:21). There is nothing natural or instinctive about submitting yourself to someone else, even if it is your spouse. The human instinct jealously guards control over one's own life. But Stephanie and I quickly discovered that the fight for control in marriage is toxic, and the way out is mutual submission. Rather than focus on our feelings and impulses, rather than measuring our arguments in wins and losses, and rather than nursing our past hurts and hang-ups, we chose instead to concentrate our efforts on submitting ourselves first to Christ, and then to each other, and let the chips fall where they may. It saved our marriage! We discovered how to love each other even during those times when we didn't like each other.

Close personal relationships are a challenge.

Intimacy requires revealing and accepting short-comings, which is never easy. In every intimate relationship you discover something you dislike, if not hate, about the other person. Like the woman who went back to her eye doctor to return a pair of glasses. "What seems to the problem?" asked the nurse. To which the woman growled, "I want to return these glasses. My husband still isn't seeing things my way."

I know of no marriage, friendship, or partner-ship that doesn't experience a rough patch because of the discovery of something disagreeable. There are no bromides, quick fixes, or easy answers for loving those we don't like. But there are indeed answers, and through Scripture we'll examine the solutions Jesus offers.

I. The Easy Way Versus God's Way

The easiest thing to do with people we dislike is to simply get rid of them. Disposable marriages and temporary friendships are a way of life in our culture. Few would have criticized my friend who wrote of his alcoholic wife if he had given up on his marriage and gotten a divorce. And there were times in Stephanie's and my first two years of mar-riage that divorce looked tempting. BUT God has a better way than simply removing difficult people we don't like from our lives.

To approach difficult people, Jesus began with the following perspective.

> "If you love those who love you, what credit is
> that to you?"
>
> > *Luke* 6:32

Here Jesus reminds us that there is no virtue in
loving the loveable. It's natural and easy to love
those who are sweet and beautiful. It's hard and
unnatural to love the miserable old crank. And
yet Jesus' prescription for a full and satisfying life
is the same for everyone: "Love your neighbor as
yourself." Obviously, the word "neighbor" includes
those you like AND those you dislike. Here's an
illustration.

I was in Kasitu, Uganda in 2004 where I met
a group of people I'm embarrassed to say I didn't
like. There, desperate children were in my face
demanding money at every turn. At first my heart
went out to them. But after days and days of their
relentless demands, I could not help but dislike
their incessant voices drowning my own thoughts.
I could not stop myself from disliking their relentless hounding. The smallness of my heart was dis-
maying, but not surprising. If my own life experience has taught me anything about myself it is that
I am not nearly as loving as I would like to think.
Even so, Jesus' prescription is still the same. A fulfilling life includes loving our neighbors—both the
loveable AND the unlovable.

This creates a dilemma. We know that the ultimate solution to all relational problems is love, but
the evidence is that each of us has a limited capac-

ity for loving others, especially those we don't like. We know that love is the answer, but we can't always do it. We don't get into trouble because we don't know the answer. We get into trouble because we just don't do it. So what's the solution?

II. A Different Kind of Love

A wise old teacher once offered me a bit of wisdom about love which made a lasting impression: "You don't have to like 'em to love 'em." At the time I thought this an odd statement. After all, how can you love someone if you don't first like them? Isn't liking someone the first step in the process toward love? Well, the answer depends on what kind of love you're talking about. There are, after all, different kinds of love. The love of friendship requires us first to like someone before loving them. But this isn't the kind of love of which Jesus speaks when He commands "love your neighbor." No, the love to which Jesus calls us is very different and quite specific.

The Bible claims that when the seed of God's Spirit is planted in our hearts a new kind of love grows. It is not romantic love. Neither is it brotherly love. It is unconditional love—the love that loves the unlovable. It is not a love we are born with, so it is not instinctive. Nor are we able to learn it on our own, so it is not developmental. It is a supernatural, spiritually inspired, unconditional love. It is love for the unlovable. The Bible describes it in this way:

"Love is patient and kind; it is not jealous or boastful; it is not arrogant or rude. Love does not insist on its own way; it is not irritable or resentful; it does not rejoice in wrong, but rejoices in the right. Love bears all things, believes all things, hopes all things, endures all things."

1 *Corinthians* 13:4–8

This love is an entirely different kind of love than what we in the 21st century are used to considering. We're used to hearing about romantic love, where "Access Hollywood" serves up all the latest gossip about the movie world's latest love interests. Occasionally, something is offered about brotherly love in movies. *Amazing Grace*, the incredible story of William Wilberforce, was such a movie. But almost never is anything expressed about unconditional love—the love that loves those we don't like.

The New Testament, however, is filled with accounts of unconditional love, like the story of the Prodigal Son. The story describes the relationship between a father and his two sons. The younger son didn't care if his father lived or died; he only wanted his money, so he demanded an early inheritance. Amazingly enough, the father granted the boy's request, and gave him his portion of the estate. The boy then quickly left home for a foreign land to squander his father's hard-earned money. He was not a particularly likeable boy by any standard.

Predictably, the money soon ran out, and famine struck the land so that the lad was forced to hire himself out to a farmer feeding his pigs (bad work for a good Jewish boy). After several weeks of near starvation, the young man realized just how good he had it in his father's house. He rehearsed an apology and set out for home. Days later when he approached his family farm, it was his father who saw his son first silhouetted against the late afternoon sky. There wasn't a moment of hesitation, for love exploded the father out of his seat. Abandoning all reserve and dignity, he picked up the skirts of his robe and ran, not stopping until he threw himself in a heap of kisses upon his son. It never occurred to the father not to take his son back. The lad may not have been particularly likable, but the heart of his father was lifted high above any human limits by an unconditional love.

This then is the challenge: To go beyond the limits of our own hearts to love those we don't like. To love the selfish child and the indifferent spouse. To love the cruel boss and the nasty neighbor. To love the pedophile and the terrorist. For believers and non-believers alike, left to our own resources, we just can't do it. It's not a question of motivation. We can think of lots of good reasons for loving those we don't like; we just can't do it. It's a simple matter of capacity. We have neither the emotional nor spiritual capacity to love those we don't like. This is why we need God's help. Only God has the power to take us beyond ourselves.

This, by the way, is nothing more than basic Christianity. The Christian dies to self so Christ might live. There are different ways to express the notion of dying to self: acknowledging our limitations, accepting our powerlessness, coming to an end of ourselves, hitting bottom. Whatever we call it, the essence of the experience is the same. Our stubborn insistence to live life our own way must die, whereupon we hand over control to God. Again, giving control to God can be expressed in different ways: inviting Jesus to live in our hearts, to be born again, turning over a new leaf, receiving new life, experiencing salvation. Whatever we call it, the meaning is the same—it is to give up on our limited capacity in favor of God's limitless capacity to love.

A capacity to love those we don't like is critically important in today's angry world. Let me offer some examples. Evangelical Christians are accused of disliking homosexuals while homosexuals are accused of returning the favor, and together the warring factions are breaking apart ancient denominations. Political conservatives and liberals dislike each other, and shun the possibility of reconciliation on many critical issues. The poor distrust the rich, and the rich to do their best to distance themselves from the poor. The Baptists are suspicious of the Episcopalians, who ridicule the Pentecostals, who dismiss the Methodists, who aren't welcome to commune with the Catholics, who disagree with the Presbyterians. Globally, the situation is just as contentious where politics, economics, and military might reflect the likes and dislikes of nations. America distrusts Syria, whic hates Israel, which resents the Palestinians, who in turn distrust America. At the same time, the threats of nuclear annihilation, biological catastrophe, and global warming place the very survival of our planet upon our ability to get along with those we don't like. Dr. Martin Luther King Jr. summarized our precarious circumstances well when he observed, "We can live together as brothers or we can die together as fools."

Astonishingly enough, the Bible has zero concern for how we *feel* about other people—whether we like or dislike them. In today's world, we spend enormous amounts of time, money, and energy in an effort to be liked by others. But the Bible generally, and Jesus specifically, wastes no time on popularity. Instead, Jesus focuses on the love that loves the unlovable.

Consider how Jesus felt when He was arrested and abandoned by all His followers in the Garden of Gethsemane. How much do you think Jesus liked the disciples who fled Him in His hour of need? Doubtless He was disappointed and didn't feel particularly warm toward them, but Jesus didn't waste a word on the matter. Or when Jesus had the flesh whipped off His back by Roman guards, how much do you think He liked them? Not a bit, I'm sure. Even so He never rebuked them, but stayed focused on His mission of love. And when Jesus was forced to carry His Cross to His own execution, how much do you think He liked Pontius Pilot, or King Herrod who arranged His death? I'm confident not at all. But that didn't stop Him from offering Himself as a sacrifice on their behalf!

We've all heard a thousand times over that Jesus loves us. But just because the Lord loves us doesn't mean that He always likes us. I'm quite sure that the Lord doesn't find us particularly likeable when we are cruel to our spouse or violent with our children. Thankfully, He doesn't need to like us to love us. Indeed, He loves us best when we are least likeable. When we are at our most selfish and self-absorbed, He works all the more to reach us. This is an utterly different kind of love than what we presume to understand.

As parents it is especially important to love our children when they aren't particularly likable—when they talk back, when they disobey, and when they're selfish and rude. The same can be said for all relationships. Some circumstances demand us to do loving things for people we despise. Indeed, people need love most when they are least lovable. Fortunately, the Bible never commands us to *like* our neighbor. We don't have to like our mother-in-law to make sure she sees her grandchildren regularly. The boss at work doesn't need to be liked to be respected. And neither do spouses have to be liked before loving things are done on their behalf.

But who can do it? Who can love someone they don't like?

I. The Example of Abraham Lincoln

A bad man hates those who like him.

A normal man likes those who like him.

A better man will tolerate those who dislike him.

But a great man will love his enemy.

—Anonymous

Once such great man in history is Abraham Lincoln, widely considered to be American's finest president. What isn't commonly remembered is just how unpopular he was during most of his presidency. His approval ratings were deplorable throughout much of his administration. Had General Sherman not taken Atlanta in September of 1864, Lincoln probably wouldn't have been reelected. Amazingly, his unpopularity wasn't just with the general public. The majority of his own cabinet despised him at the beginning of his term. Even some of Lincoln's hand-picked generals dismissed him as a backwoods buffoon. Yet with all the unpopularity and disrespect, Lincoln rarely lost his composure or compassion for others. He was a man of great faith who possessed a superhuman reservoir of poise and unconditional love. One story in particular illustrates his capacity to love the unlovable.

It was late one night in Washington D.C., but President Lincoln had an urgent need to speak with the general of the Potomac Army–General

McClellan. Lincoln and his Secretary of State, William Seward, walked from the White House to the general's nearby home, where they were greeted at the door by the general's butler. The president was informed that the general had yet to return home, but that he was expected shortly. Lincoln indicated he would be pleased to wait, so the butler escorted the president and secretary to the parlor, where they sat waiting. When at last General McClellan arrived home, his butler promptly informed him of Lincoln's presence. But the General passed by the parlor's open door and went straight up the stairs to his private quarters. After another half-hour wait, President Lincoln sent the butler to remind the General he was wanted, but the President was informed that General McClellan was asleep. Secretary Seward was outraged, but Lincoln simply said, "I will hold McClellan's horse if victory can be achieved." Without saying more, the President and Secretary left, never to mention the slight.

Abraham Lincoln had good reason to dislike such disrespectful people. He was dismissed as incompetent within his own administration, caricatured as a frontier fool in the press, and vilified as a blood-thirsty war monger by many in the church and in the peace movement. No doubt, Lincoln privately didn't like the people who enjoyed slandering his name and character. But he wasted no energy in trying to like them. Instead, he was generous with his prayers and praise and did everything he could to encourage those who had difficult jobs to do.

Mr. Lincoln read regularly and deeply from the Scriptures, which no doubt sustained him during impossible times. No man has such wells of unconditional love naturally. They are grown by God within the heart of a man or woman who welcomes God's spirit and cooperates while God grows and harvests His spiritual fruit of love.

III. How Do We Love The Unlovable?

So how do we do it? What are the action steps to love someone when we don't like them? How do we allow the Spirit of Christ to lift us beyond the limitations of our human hearts?

First, *don't waste energy trying to like someone you don't.* There is nothing unchristian about not liking someone. We are called to love our neighbor, not like them. I doubt Pilate was particularly likeable to Jesus. And the Bible tells us that the Apostle Paul quarreled with the Apostle Peter, after which they may not have been the best of friends. Don't waste your time forcing yourself to like someone. Do loving things for them with patience and kindness. Love them as you would love yourself. After all, you don't always like yourself, but that probably doesn't stop you from caring for yourself.

In our first two years of marriage, Stephanie's and my fight for control created plenty of reasons to dislike each other, and we wasted lots of mental energy convincing ourselves to feel differently. We didn't want to feel badly about the other person, but we didn't always feel good, so often we just felt numb. We were coming to terms with the realization that we felt some hatred. And as long as we focused on our hurt feelings, it just got worse. But when we asked God to take us beyond our feelings, the healing began.

The first point is simple. Don't waste your time and effort trying to feel something you don't. You don't have to like 'em to love 'em.

Second. The most generous thing you can do for those you don't like is to *lift them up to God in prayer.* Pray not that they change, but for God's blessing to fall upon their life. If we don't like someone, there is little we can do to change him or her. But there is everything we can do to change our attitude toward them.

Even if Jesus didn't always like His disciples, it didn't stop Him from praying for them. Jesus never stopped praying for the blessing of God's unconditional love to overflow into their hearts.

Do you have an unlikable boss? The most practical thing you can do is to pray for God's blessing in his/her life. Are you unhappy with your spouse? Pray that God will continue to soften your heart toward him/her.

Recently, I was asked if I liked everyone in the Church I serve as pastor. The answer is "no." Churches are complicated places. They attract the healthy and the unhealthy alike. They're supposed to. The great reformer Martin Luther described churches as "hospitals for the spiritually sick." As a result, they collect all sorts of characters, some of whom are not particularly likeable. Even so, people come to church because they need all the love and care they can get. As a pastor, I may not like everyone in my church, but thankfully it's not necessary to be effective in prayer and service on their behalf. God directs us to lift the concerns of others up to Him, especially those in special need.

Third, regardless of how you feel, *do loving things for those you dislike.* Serve their interests. Accept their concerns as your concerns, and do something about it.

Even when Jesus was crucified, He didn't stop loving the unlikable. While He hung on the cross, He offered salvation to the thief who hung beside Him. Remarkably, He even prayed for forgiveness and mercy for those responsible for His death. And then He did the the most loving thing of all. He offered Himself as a sacrifice to pay for our sins, yours and mine. The human race may not have seemed very likable to Jesus, but He loved us, quite literally, to death. As the Word says:

> "But God shows His love for us in that while we were yet sinners Christ died for us."
>
> *Romans* 5:8

Remember, unconditional love is less about what we feel and more about what we believe and do.

My marriage took a major turn for the better when I came to appreciate that what I do supercedes how I feel. As a self-absorbed member of the baby-boomer generation, I grew up with the presumption that my feelings dictated what I did. If I liked you I would act accordingly, and if I didn't, again I would act accordingly. But in the Gospels I discovered that Jesus Himself never lived this way, nor did He preach a message that was grounded in how anyone felt—least of all how He felt. It was quite the opposite. Jesus was all about doing loving things in spite of how He felt, and from that behavior would spring an irrepressible and quite inexplicable love. By Faith, both my wife and I decided to take a chance on this approach—to submit ourselves to each other and do loving things for the other regardless of how we felt. Rather than focusing on justice for hurt feelings, we instead focused on doing gracious things for the other regardless of the "score." At first it was wooden and awkward. We could tell that the other was "trying hard." But eventually the graces we bestowed upon each other piled up and buried our wounds.

IV. Begin With Me

My friend with the alcoholic wife had a big problem that his best intentions and efforts could not solve. Human nature is just too limited to love the unlovable, even when we want to. This is why St. Paul wrote, "I know what the right thing to do is, but I just can't do it." Inevitably, it is necessary for God's Spirit to plant itself in our hearts. The Scripture is only too aware of human limitations, and how God uses our weaknesses as occasions to supply His strength.

" ... Power is made perfect in weakness ... so that the power of Christ may dwell in me."

2 Corinthians 12:9

We quickly reach our own limitations when loving the unlovely, and our need for divine assistance becomes obvious. Fortunately, God is only too eager to supply our need, but of course we have to do it in His way and in His time. When we allow Him to plant Himself at the center of our hearts, we soon discover new growth within us, growth that resembles neither the passions of our own hearts nor the impulses of our spirits. Instead, we discover a cool breeze blowing against the advance of our self-centeredness and a new warmth that concerns itself for the well-being of others. It is a climate well suited for the growth of God's unconditional love, which springs forth from the seed of His Divine Spirit. As it grows, we are privileged to enjoy the heights and depths, width and breadth of God's unconditional love and the power to love that unlovable person, just as Jesus did.

Jesus was once approached by a mob dragging a terrified woman caught in the act of adultery. If anyone is easy to dislike, it is an unfaithful spouse, and evidently everyone in town disliked her enough to look forward to her death by stoning. The mob, which probably included her crazed husband, threw her down before Jesus and demanded a guilty verdict. But Jesus knelt and wrote with His finger in the dirt, and then rose up to say, "Let he who is without sin cast the first stone." One by one, the woman's accusers dropped their rocks and left until the woman was alone before Jesus.

He said to her, "Woman, is there no one left to condemn you?"

She said, "No one, Lord."

"Then neither do I condemn you; go, and do not sin again." (John 8:1–11).

Notice that Jesus did not waste time and energy trying to like either the woman who sinned or the mob which condemned. Frankly, neither was likable that day. Instead, He did the loving thing for both. He shared His heart, out of which grew an astonishing love, a love which was neither conditional nor judgmental.

Many of the relational problems we face can be resolved by an overflowing supply of God's unconditional love. It breaks down walls that separate and heals the hurts that torment. It enables us to go beyond our heart's earthbound limits and taps into the extravagant generosity of God's heart. It is just as Jesus said,

> "With men it is impossible, but not with God,
> *for all things are possible with God.*"
>
> *Mark* 10:27

This love for the unlovely is rare. It is always astonishing when it is experienced. But this is not to say that it is out of most people's reach. It is available to anyone. It has nothing to do with intelligence, education, family background, or religious affiliation. Its only requirement is a willingness to die to self and the desire for Christ to live in and through your heart.

V. Conclusion

My dear friend with the alcoholic wife paid a high emotional price for staying in his marriage. It wasn't the choice that everyone would make. But choosing to stay forced him to go beyond the limits of his heart to love the wife who was no longer likable. To remain sane and healthy, he had to cultivate God's unconditional love, which has made him a truly remarkable human being. Indeed, one might be tempted to call him a saint. He, of course, would steadfastly deny it. But it is just the sort of thing saints do—love beyond normal limits. And "saint" is precisely the description God promises to give us when we give Him the opportunity to grow His spiritual fruit in our own hearts.

Group Study:
You Don't Have To Like 'Em to Love 'Em
(90 minutes)

Introduction (5 minutes)
Briefly:
- Share your names & backgrounds
- Share in 12 words or less what you would DO if your 19 year old child demanded that you give them their inheritance.

Opening Discussion/Warm Up: (5 minutes)
With a partner (one on one) discuss how the expression "familiarity breeds contempt" is true and untrue. Share a time when circumstances pushed you to do loving things for someone you didn't particularly like at the time. How did you feel during and after the experience?

I. The Easy Way Verses the Hard Way (5 min.)
a. Reassemble and read aloud Luke 6:32. Discuss how it challenges the notion of "disposable relationships":
"If you love those who love you, what credit is that to you?"
b. Is it possible to love someone if they don't love you?
c. Is it possible to love someone without first liking them?

II. A Different Kind of Love: (30 minutes)

a. The ancient Greek language has four different words for love:
   - i. Eros—romantic love
   - ii. Philia–brotherly love
   - iii. Storgie–acquaintance love
   - iv. Agape–unconditional love

b. Four Corners: Choose a different "love" for each corner of your room (i.e.–one corner for *eros*, another corner for *philia*, etc ...). Have participants go to the corner/love they are most comfortable with, and have them discuss with those in their same corner why they've chosen that particular love.

c. Next, have participants go to the corner/love they are least comfortable with, and have them discuss with those in their same corner why they are uncomfortable with that particular love.

d. Reassemble: The Bible defines *agape* love in 1 Corinthians 13. Read the passage aloud–add up the number of words used to describe love. List them. Is there any mention of emotion in the definition 1 Cor 13 provides?

"Love is patient and kind; love is not jealous or boastful; it is not arrogant or rude. Love does not insist on its own way; it is not irritable or resentful; it does not rejoice in wrong, but rejoices in the right. Love bears all things, believes all things, hopes all things, and endures all things. Love never ends."

1 *Corinthians* 13:4–8

    e. According to 1 Corinthians. 13 is emotion/feeling necessary for *agape* love?

    f. If love is the first of the spiritual fruit (Galatians 5:22) does that mean that it is also the most important? What does 1 Corinthians 13:13 seem to suggest?

"... Now faith, hope, and love abide, these three; and the greatest of these is love (agape)."

1 *Corinthians* 13:13

III. How Do We Love the Unloveable? (15 minutes)

    a. Does the Bible command us to "like" people or to "love" them? Describe the difference.

    b. Where is relational success more likely? Is it to pray for an unlikable person to change, OR pray that our attitude toward that person change?

    c. The Bible commands us to "love our neighbor." Does that mean we are to feel a certain way or act a certain way toward our neighbor?

    d. According to Romans 5:8, does God wait

to like us before He does loving things
for us?

"But God shows His love for us in that while
we were yet sinners Christ died for us."

Romans 5:8

IV. Begin with Me: (15 minutes)

a. According to the Bible is it acceptable
to dislike another person? Do you think
Jesus always liked His disciples? What
does Mark 8:31–33 suggest?

"Then Jesus began to teach them that the
Son of Man must undergo great suffering, and be rejected by the elders, the
chief priests, and the scribes, and be
killed, and after three days rise again. He
said all this quite openly. And Peter took
Him aside and began to rebuke Him. But
turning and looking at His disciples, He
rebuked Peter and said, "Get behind me,
Satan! For you are setting your mind not
on divine things but on human things.""

b. When loving an unlikable person is beyond us
how does the message of 2ⁿᵈ Corinthians 12:9
help?

" ... power is made perfect in weakness ... so
that the power of Christ may dwell in me."

2 *Corinthians* 12:9

V. The Example of Abraham Lincoln:
   (10 minutes)
   a. Show a portrait of Lincoln.
   b. What are the emotions his face seems to express?
   c. Abraham Lincoln has often been referred to as America's most spiritual president. How did President Lincoln exemplify the attributes of *agape* love as defined in 1 Corinthians 13?

"Love is patient and kind; love is not jealous or boastful; it is not arrogant or rude. Love does not insist on its own way; it is not irritable or resentful; it does not rejoice in wrong, but rejoices in the right. Love bears all things, believes all things, hopes all things, endures all things. Love never ends."

1 Corinthians 13:4–8

   d. If you were to become president of the United States would it be necessary for you to love people you didn't like? Is this unconditional love necessary in your life now?
   e. What are you going to do cultivate the growth of God's love?

IV. Wrap Up: (5 minutes)
   a. Share prayer requests within the group
   b. Confirm the time and location of the next group study.
   c. Close by reading out loud the following prayer:

Dear God,

We thank You for bringing us together for this fellowship. We pray that through this study You will help us move beyond the limits of our personal likes and dislikes. May You supernaturally grow within our hearts, and empower us to love the unlovable.

We pray too that You will help us to love ourselves when we are less than likeable, and inspire us to action with deeds that serve the best interests of our family, friends, and neighbors regardless of how we feel about them. Help us to do loving things Lord, the kind that bring You the honor and glory You deserve. We submit ourselves to You Lord, and in Your Holy Name we pray. Amen.

CHAPTER TWO: JOY

Joy Has A Crazy Cousin

Mark Twain wrote what many believe to be the great American novel: *Huckleberry Finn*. But great as Twain was, he was no choir boy. His vice you may wonder? Cuss'n. He loved to cuss like a sailor. And His wife? She couldn't stand it. She did her best to censor his crude language, but she rarely succeeded. On one memorable occasion, Twain cut himself shaving and he cussed a blue streak. When he stopped, his wife thought she'd shame him by repeating word for word exactly what he had said. Of course, out of her mouth, the words sounded simply ridiculous. Twain listened attentively and then replied with a sly smile, "You have the words, my dear, but I'm afraid you'll never master the tune"[1]

'The words but not the tune.' I'm afraid this describes too many of today's christians–believers who have the words of Jesus in their head, but not the Gospel tune in their heart. According to *USA Today*[2] 87% of Americans consider themselves "spiritual people," yet many feel joyless. The Christian life in particular is experienced by too many as solemn and glum - a black robe, a long face, and a flickering candle in the dark. But the Christian Faith began with unimaginable joy. When Jesus rose from the dead the earth trembled, the angels sang, His disciples rejoiced, and ever since joy has been the Faith's melody and harmony. Indeed, the scripture goes so far as to promise joy to the followers of Christ.

> "…ask, and you will receive, that your **JOY** may be full."

John 16:24

Can it be that joy is closer than we imagine? Have we simply overlooked one of joy's hiding places? Let me show you one surprising place you can start.

I. Joy's Crazy Cousin
Let me begin with a digression. I wonder how many of you have a crazy cousin. You know the relative who causes the family regular embarrassment. President Jimmy Carter had his brother Billy Carter. Remember "Billy Beer"?

I had some crazy cousins who lived in the Pittsburgh,

PA. area when I was growing up. They were two old maid sisters who were absolutely brilliant, with more education than I ever dreamed of achieving, but lived as recluses in a ramshackle trailer deep in the woods. While that by itself may not sound so peculiar, add 27 cats and no electricity and you've got one sure recipe for crazy. You couldn't get within ten yards of their trailer without the smell of stale cat urine knocking you down. Like it or not, these were my crazy cousins.

Well it turns out JOY has a crazy cousin of its own ... one most of us would never suspect, and this cousin plays an essential role in our ability to experience joy. You see joy's crazy cousin is suffering, and surprisingly enough we can't fully welcome joy into our life without also welcoming her cousin suffering, because as the scriptures testify, joy and suffering are closely related. From the Old Testament to the New, God's Word relates these two concepts.

> Weeping may linger for the night, but **JOY** comes in the morning."
>
> *Psalm* 30:5

> " ... your sorrow will be turned to **JOY**."
>
> *John* 16:20

> "Count it all **JOY** when you meet with various trials."
>
> *James* 1:2

No doubt about it, joy and suffering are related in scripture. But why?

Have you ever noticed that some of the most joyful people you know are those who have suffered greatly? It's been said that those "closest to suffering have the most powerful joy"[1] While this concept is counter intuitive, nonetheles it is true that joyful people are not those with the best circumstances but those with the best hearts.

A practical application of this principle is worship. If you want to attend a joy-filled worship service on Sunday morning, where would you go? I know where I would go. I'd go to the poorest section of town to a Church whose pastor and people have suffered a great deal. I'd go where they raise their arms in praise, clap their hands in adoration, stomp their feet with expectation, and "get happy" during the service. These folks don't postpone joy. They don't wait for their circumstances to get better. They let whatever joy the Lord offers pour into their suffering hearts. They may be closest to suffering, yet their joy is also the most powerful. And what kind of music will they sing there? Gospel music of course. Gospel music is the most joyful music there is, and interestingly enough it developed in the blast furnace of slavery ... the worst of human suffering.

Yes, this spiritual principle has always been true: joy and suffering are closely related. Don't get me wrong. I'm not suggesting suffering is good. It isn't. It's a curse. But our response to suffering can serve God's purposes. Suffering can force our hearts to grow large enough to choose hope over despair. When we do this, we truly become possessed of a Christ-like joy.

The alternative, of course, is not to suffer. But I don't know many saints who developed a deep understanding of God without suffering. An easy life tends to breed a superficial life, one surprisingly void of joy.

So let me ask you: To whom would you go when you need a word of hope and inspiration? Would you go to the person who has never suffered ... who walked down easy street all their life? Or would you pay a visit to the person who has been through the fires of hell, and who came out the other end still holding on to God—somene who earned their PhD from the school of hard knocks, and whose suffering taught them that nothing in all creation could separate them from the love of God in Christ Jesus?

Joy is related to suffering, and if you want to invite joy into your life, you've also got to welcome her cousin suffering, because hard times are always part of the climb to the summit of joy.

Could this be why some Christians don't experience much joy? Because they just aren't willing to spend any time with suffering. Many decide it isn't worth it. Given the choice between a life filled with great suffering and joy, or a vanilla suburban life of minimal suffering and little joy, the average person will choose the vanilla life almost every time. They would rather avoid the pain than experience the joy.

One need look no further than Christ for the ultimate example. Jesus chose to leave the comforts of heaven to suffer the cross. But in doing so He composed the joyful tune of the Gospel. This is how the Bible describes it:

> "Jesus ... who for the JOY that was set before Him endured the cross."
>
> *Hebrews* 12:3

So why are joy and suffering related? If God loves us, why must we suffer as we climb the spiritual mountain? The answer is simple. The joy of the one who climbs Mt. Everest is going to be infinitely greater than the joy of the one who climbs sugar hill. Something deep in the soul of each man and woman requires a challenge and a purpose. If everything in our lives went just the way we wanted, our health was perfect, our studies a breeze, our marriages easy, our children obedient, and our careers satisfying, our lives would not be glorious. They would be banal. Nothing of our character would be developed. Our spirit would be spineless and bored. The day we have nothing to suffer for is the day we have nothing to love and live for. Often it is in the midst of this suffering that we discover what we are, and *whose* we are. This is why the brother of Jesus wrote the following words:

> "Count it all JOY, my brothers and sisters, when you meet various trials, for you know that the testing of your faith produces steadfastness. And let steadfastness have its full effect, that you may be perfect and complete ... "
>
> *James* 1:2–4

It's just as the old saying goes: "The hardest steel is forged in the hottest fire." The souls of the saints are not molded in easy times. It is their suffering that melts their hearts so that God can reshape them for joy.

The following letter from a Naval officer observes how surprised by joy he was while serving in Baghdad in some very tragic and frightening circumstances. He writes:

"I was in downtown Baghdad for nine months and getting mortared almost every day. Each day could literally have been my last. We took a rocket hit at work shortly after I arrived that killed two of my colleagues. We lived in trailers packed in trenches reminiscent of World War I, with sandbags piled ten feet high. Daily car bombs cracked our windows as they sent terrifying, earthquake-like shock waves through the compound. Bullets occasionally ripped through trailer roofs, the mess-hall roof, and even through the roof of our small chapel. Machine-gun battles, often several at a time, could be heard just outside our gates at all hours of the day and night. Every time we went outside we were in body armor and helmets, while carrying our weapons. My trailermate and I read our Bibles every night and prayed on our knees in the morning. Once we went for numerous days without showers after the insurgents disrupted our water supply. It was hot and dusty much of the time. The air smelled of smoke and rot. Oddly, I have never been happier in my adult life than when I was in Baghdad! My feelings of joy surprised me greatly, and came from the knowledge that I was part of a noble mission to bring order to chaos and introduce democracy to the long-suffering people of Iraq."

My point here is not political. I only wish to illustrate that joy can come to us in the most unexpected places, and under the worst of circumstances. Indeed, joy can thrive in suffering.

II. A Touch of Heaven

The Bible's most joyful book is the Book of Philippians. In its four short pages the words "joy" and "rejoice" are used no less than 14 times. One might assume the writer was a happy man in good circumstances. In truth, Philippians was written by St. Paul while he was in prison at the mercy of sadistic prison guards, sexual predators, rampant sickness, and starvation. Here is how the Scripture describes Paul's circumstances:

" ... they threw them (Paul and Silas) into prison, charging the jailor to keep them safely. Having received this charge, he (the jailer) put them into the inner prison and fastened their feet in the stocks. But about midnight Paul and Silas were praying and singing hymns to God, and the prisoners were listening to them ... "

Acts 16:22–25

In a dark, damp, cold, and dangerous dungeon St. Paul still had the joy to sing out loud the Gospel tune.

Ironically, the Christian faith has always prevailed, not because of its moral superiority, but because of its enduring joy. And today Christianity remains contagious because of that same joy. Through the centuries Christian men and women have confounded their opponents and detractors with hope that contradicted their circumstances. Instead of suffering dragging them down to despair, just the opposite happened. Their suffering multiplied their joy, and dumfounded all witnesses.

III. The Joy of Brother Yun:

Let me share another example of joy amidst suffering. It occurred during a communist Chinese crackdown of the Christian movement. Born in China in 1958, Brother Yun suffered torture and prison for his faith in Jesus Christ. His autobiography, *The Heavenly Man*, tells of a time when he suffered for his faith while simultaneously experiencing God's joy. Brother Yun writes:

"Nine prisoners from the men's and women's prisons in Nanyang were to face public humiliation and trial that day. I was one of them. We were driven around the town, while our crimes were read out on a loudspeaker. I was full of joy at the chance of being paraded in front of people for the sake of Jesus Christ! My heart was bursting with gladness.

"On the way to the trial I couldn't contain myself. I'd just seen Brother Huang promoted to glory, and eternity was so real to me. I sang out to God in a loud voice. The captain threatened me with his electric baton. '"Shut up, Yun! How dare you sing! If you continue to sing I'll skin you alive!"'

"All nine prisoners were chained together like animals and bundled into the back of an open truck. As the truck circled the streets a heavy rain shower suddenly came and drenched us to the bone. It was like refreshment from heaven to me. I cried aloud, 'Lord, I thirst after rains of grace! Abundantly pour out your showers of grace upon your servant!'

"I kept on singing loudly. Many people, huddled under umbrellas, stared at us in total amazement. Because we were all locals, many of the other prisoners bowed their heads in shame, not wanting to be recognized by their friends and relatives.

"There was one young woman, aged about twenty, in the back of the truck with me. Her name was Xiaowei. She was in prison because she had fought with her neighbors. Xiaowei was a Christian, but her walk with God had not been strong.

"Xiaowei was weeping as I sang. She asked me, 'Why are you so joyful during such a time as this?'

"I told her, 'How can I not be happy? This day I've been counted worthy to suffer for the name of Jesus!'

"Xiaowei's face turned red. I continue to sing aloud:

Though the whole world hates me, and friends forsake me,

Though my fleshly temple be destroyed by slander, persecution, and beatings,

I will give my life and spill my blood to please my Heavenly Father,

That wearing the crown of life I will enter the Kingdom of God!

"Xiaowei couldn't contain her tears and pulled a handkerchief from her pocket. I told her, 'Xiaowei, the Holy Spirit is grieved for you. The prodigal's return is more precious than gold. Return, your Heavenly Father is waiting for you!'

"With many tears she repented and cried out, 'O Lord, have mercy on me, a sinner! Please forgive my sins.' I prayed for her and thanked God for His mercy. She received peace and joy into her heart. Xiaowei then stood on tiptoe and wiped the tears from my eyes with her handkerchief.

"The truck continued on in the direction of my home village. Xiaowei turned to me and said, 'I heard there is a bold servant of God named Yun who lived in that village. Do you know what happened to him?'

"I chuckled and asked, 'Would you like to meet that man?'

"She replied, 'I heard his testimony from others in my Church. How could I meet him?'

"I said, 'Yun is the man talking with you now.'

"Xiaowei again broke down in tears and thanked God we'd been given a chance to meet. She held onto me as our truck continued its journey through the streets.

"All of the prisoners on the truck were totally soaked to the skin. Even the police–holding their machine guns under their rain-coats–trembled from the cold wind and driving rain. Because of their discomfort the soldiers paid little attention to us, and none of the public came out to attend our trials. The meeting was cancelled. The whole day was a failure for the authorities.

"Our chains and ropes were loosed back at the police station. All the police officers had a big meal. We were allowed to eat the leftovers when they were finished. We ate together, thanking the Lord for the rich fellowship we had enjoyed that day."[2]

IV. Suffering Transformed to Joy!
Yes, joy and suffering are related. It has always

been true. The grape must first be crushed before the wine can flow. A grain of wheat is first crushed before it is eaten. It is just as the prophet Habakkuk described it:

> "Though the fig tree does not blossom,
>   Nor fruit be on the vines,
> The produce of the olive fail
>   And the fields yield no food,
> The flock be cut off from the fold
>   And there be no herd in the stalls,
> Yet I will rejoice in the Lord,
>   I will JOY in the God of my salvation
> God, the Lord is my strength;
>   He makes my feet like hinds feet.
> He makes me tread upon my high places."
>
> *Habakkuk 3:17–19*

Not one of Jesus' disciples escaped extreme suffering and yet the record of each disciple's life documents an irrepressible joy strong enough to transform one of the mightiest and cruelest empires history has ever known—Rome. Their joy was rooted in the knowledge that their names were written large in the Lamb's Book of Life. Their joy was rooted in the belief that they were doing exactly what God created them to do - that they had abandoned their earthly pursuits for heavenly ones. Their joy was rooted in the understanding that their lives had transcended far beyond themselves.

What's more, the suffering of each disciple helped them to discern their life's true purpose and meaning. Suffering helped them (and helps us) to listen more closely, and yield more completely to the voice of God. Why? Because we tend to subvert God's purposes with our own agendas and ambitions. But when we suffer we eventually reach the end of ourselves, and at last submit our wills to God.

Had Christ not entered their lives the twelve apostles certainly would have suffered less trial and tribulation. But their lives? What lasting meaning would their lives have had? Would they have lived and died in meaningless tedium? As it was, they were transformed from mere fishermen, tax collectors, and soldiers into the heralds of the greatest spiritual revolution of human history. These men knew joy; joy that radiated from Jerusalem to Ethiopia, and from India to Britain.

Tradition tells us that the Apostle Andrew's joy inspired him to serve as a missionary to Achaia (Southern Greece) where he was crucified. That same tradition goes on to say that he hung alive on the cross for two days, all the while exhorting spectators to come to Christ! The Apostle Bartholomew's joy is said to have moved him to preach in India, Mesopotamia, Persia, Egypt, Phrygia and on the shores of the Black Sea. According to tradition, he was flayed alive and crucified, head downward as punishment for having converted the King of Armenia to the Christian faith. The Apostle James the Lesser was martyred in Jerusalem by being thrown from a pinnacle of the Temple. He was then stoned and beaten with clubs and fuller's mallets, all the while praying for his attackers.

Common men and women simply don't do such uncommon things unless motivated by something extraordinary! The Apostle Paul, who himself was beheaded in Rome for Christ, writes of their motivation:

> "We rejoice in our sufferings, knowing that suffering produces endurance, and endurance produces character, and character produces hope, and hope does not disappoint us, because God's love has been poured into our hearts through the Holy Spirit which has been given to us"
>
> *Romans* 5:3–5

The Apostle Paul states clearly that when God's love is poured into the human heart the worst of human suffering is transformed into the surprise of God's joy. This was true for each of the Apostles, and it can be just as true for you!

V. Why Is This Good News?

And why is this good news—that joy is so closely connected with suffering? Perhaps this story touches the heart of the answer:

The 16-year old son of one of my childhood friends died tragically of a drug overdose recently. Her son was handsome, popular at school, a golden child. Unfortunately, having choosen the wrong way to celebrate with friends, he's now dead. His

mother and father's suffering is worse than anything they'd ever imagined. Just when they think
they've hit bottom, it gets still worse. But the good
news of the gospel is that my friend and her husband are now excellent candidates for joy. I know
this is counter intuitive, but it is how joy works.
To suffer trama like the loss of a child is to lose
the desire to cling to anything except what's most
important, and joy is what's most important. In
their wretched suffering my friend and her husband
will stop chasing the world's many enticements.
Their sorrow will put a stop to their busy lifestyle
like a punch to the stomach. Doubled over, hardly
able to breath, unable to move, they will finally
be still enough for the Lord to approach. God can
then offer what they least expect—joy.

All across the world people suffer horrible
wounds to their heart and soul. In anguish they
wonder if they will ever recover. Such people are all
excellent candidates for joy. In their suffering, joy
moves toward them. It is not at all what we expect,
but in the pit of our worst suffering we make some
surprising discoveries. We learn that the worst of
death cannot overcome the best of life. We learn
that no matter what the trial or tribulation nothing can separate us from the love of God in Christ
Jesus. We learn that love pursues us much more
persistently than we ourselves pursue it!

As the scripture reassures us,

"Weeping may linger for the night, but **JOY** comes in the morning."

Psalm 30:5

Counter-intuitive? Yes. But like many of the assurances of scripture, they are counter to the asumptions of the world.

The world presumes that when you suffer something is wrong. But the Bible has a different perspective. It maintains that suffering might well be evidence that you are working against the tide of the world's darkness. This is why the Bible says, "Count it all joy when you meet with various trials..." God's word promises that the people of God will suffer, for light can have no fellowship with darkness. So if you are not suffering, you might want to ask yourself why. And if you are suffering, take heart. You may well be much closer to God's promised joy than you think. For as the Scripture promises,

"Truly, truly I say to you, you will weep and lament, but the world will rejoice; you will be sorrowful, but your sorrow will turn into joy."

John 16:20

I don't know about you, but this sounds like a Gospel tune that I can sing!

And the Gospel doesn't end there. Indeed its news gets still better. It assures us that even though joy and suffering are linked, nonetheless Jesus has already absorbed for us the worst part of our suffering. As the Scripture declares, Jesus was a "man of suffering, acquainted with grief..." His reward for the purity of His life was to be crucified sadistically. But upon that Cross, Jesus absorbed all human sin onto Himself. When He descended into hell, He absorbed whatever sufferings were due each of us. In so doing He took upon Himself the worst of our suffering. This means that instead of a pending judgment on the other side of our death, we now have an inexpressible and glorious joy. On the other side of death, we have a radiant, transcendent, glorious, eternal joy awaiting us! My friend and her husband therefore have this joy waiting for them, and it is the same joy that has already been offered to their son. And you? What about you? This joy is offered to you. Do you trust God? That is the only requirement. Trust Him.

Like I said, this is a Gospel tune that anyone can sing!

Group Study:
Joy's Crazy Cousin (90 minutes)

Introduction (5 minutes)
Briefly:

- Remind one another of your names
- Share with the group whether you come from a big or small family.
- Share with the group whether you are considered "normal" in your family.

Opening Discussion/Warm Up: (10 minutes)

> "In this world you will have trouble, but fear not, I have overcome the world."
>
> *John* 16:33

Are these words of joy, resignation, protest, or delusion? Assign a corner of the room for each word and have each participant go to one of the corners, and explain their choice.

I. Joy's Crazy Cousin (20 minutes)

a. Share descriptions of some of the crazy relatives in your family.

b. Does it seem odd that the Bible would relate suffering with joy in the following verses?

> "Count it all **JOY** when you meet with various trials."
>
> *James* 1:2

"Weeping may linger for the night, but **JOY** comes in the morning."

Psalm 30:5

" ... your sorrow will be turned to **JOY**."

John 16:20

    c. Where would you go if you needed an infusion of joy in your life? Why?

    d. What's better, to live a meaningful/ exciting/purposeful life with suffering, or to live a bland/purposeless life without suffering? Divide the room in half with a glass of warm milk (bland) on one side and salsa and chips (exciting) on the other. Have each participant get out of their seats and go to the side of the room that reflects their choice. They must choose one or the other ... no straddling the middle ground! Have participants explain their choice.

II. A Touch of Heaven (20 minutes)

    a. Share with one another what you think you might be doing at midnight on your first night in jail.

    b. Read together out loud:

        " ... they threw them (Paul and Silas) into prison, charging the jailor to · keep them safely. Having received this charge, he (the jailer) put them into the inner prison and fastened their feet in the stocks. But about midnight Paul and Silas were praying and singing hymns to God, and the prisoners were listening to them ... "

Acts 16:22–25

   c. Do you think Paul and Silas were feeling joy, hoping for joy, or simply believing that joy was still possible?

   d. If joy is not circumstantial, what is its origin?

(Note: the word for "joy" in Greek *(chara)* is essentially the same word as the Greek word for "gift" *(charisma)* and "grace"– *(charis)*. Is joy more a gift and grace than a circumstance?

III. The Joy of Brother Yun (15 minutes)

   a. Have someone read the account of Brother Yun to the group.

   b. Have each person take out a small piece of paper and have them write one of two words: "trade" or "no trade."

        i. "Trade" means you would trade your life for Brother Yun's. "No trade" means you would keep your life as it is. Have each person write their choice on the paper, collect each person's choice, and tally the number for each answer. Announce the results and discuss.

ii. Discuss why you think the voting went as it did.

iii. What is the implication? Is security and comfort more important than meaning and purpose?

IV. You May Be Closer To Joy Than You Think
(15 minutes)

a. What is the source of the prophet Habakkuk's joy?

> Though the fig tree do not blossom,
>   Nor fruit be on the vines,
> The produce of the olive fail
>   And the fields yield no food,
> The flock be cut off from the fold
>   And there be no herd in the stalls,
> Yet I will rejoice in the Lord,
>   I will JOY in the God of my salvation
> God, the Lord is my strength;
>   He makes my feet like hinds feet.
> He makes me tread upon my high places.

Habakkuk 3:17–19

b. According to the Psalmist, what is the prelude to joy?

> Weeping may linger for the night, but **JOY** comes in the morning."

Psalm 30:5

    c.   According to Jesus sorrow, can turn to joy:

> "Truly, truly I say to you, you will weep and lament, but the world will rejoice; you will be sorrowful, but your sorrow will turn into joy."

John 16:20

    Have you ever witnessed sorrow turn to joy?

    d. Are you a candidate for Joy?

IV. Warm Up (5 minutes)

    a.   Share prayer requests
    b.   Confirm the time and location of the next group study.
    c.   Close by reading out loud the following Prayer:

Dear God,

We thank You for everything, even our suffering. It is in our suffering that the meaning of our lives is discerned, and that joy at last inhabits our hearts. Help us not to fear, Lord, of what is hard and painful. Give us the strength we require to persevere, and always protect us from the evil that would overwhelm us. We do understand that in this world there will be trouble, but we also trust that You have overcome the world! Amen.

CHAPTER THREE: PEACE

Sleeping Through the Storms of Hell!

How would you like to enjoy a good night's sleep? Research informs us a good sleep is not as common as one might think. Sleep deprivation affects 47 million people in America today ... almost a quarter of the adult population. Americans now average two hours less sleep a night than the average American 100 years ago. According to the 2002 Sleep In America Poll conducted by the National Sleep Foundation the average American adult now sleeps 6.9 hours a night, which isn't enough for most folk, and inevitably leads to exhaustion. There are lots of explanations for this deprivation of sleep ... late night television is an obvious suspect. But these statistics also suggest we are not a culture at peace! Too many of us have too many worries chasing us in our dreams to enjoy our rest: money worries, relationship worries, and career worries to mention three big ones. What's more, some must endure the internal civil war that rages between the spirit and flesh—purity vs lust, charity vs greed, patience vs anger. Sleep may seem a simple pleasure, but it's not at all that easy to enjoy in our world of competition, stress and strife.

In the following pages, we will take stock of God's peace, what it is, how it can be found, and better yet ... how His peace promises to find us!

I. What Peace Is and Isn't:

Let's begin with a bit of biblical history. The New Testament tells a story of peace in the Book of Acts that I find remarkable. It's the story of the apostle Peter being rescued from prison. Here is the account:

Peter was arrested by King Herod for preaching the Gospel, thrown into prison, and placed under armed guard, to await trial. Herod's intention was to murder Peter just like he executed Jesus' brother James only a few days earlier. The night before his trial, Peter was chained to two armed guards who were posted on either side of him. Now, here's what's remarkable. The New Testament tells us that through the terror of this night Peter SLEPT like a baby! This is exactly how the Scripture describes it:

> "The very night when Herod was about to
> bring him out (for trial and execution), Peter
> was SLEEPING between two soldiers, bound
> with two chains ... "

Acts 12:6

Imagine that! Peter sleeping the night before his
trial and execution! I can't speak for you, but I
would have a hard time sleeping under such circumstances. If I were in chains facing a trial for my
life the next day, I would likely be wide awake pon-
dering my options. If I did manage to fall asleep
it would be fitful at best, with terror stalking my
dreams. But the New Testament tells us that Peter
slept so soundly that an angel had to strike him on
his side to wake him up.

> "And behold, an angel of the Lord appeared,
> and a light shone in the cell; and he *struck*
> Peter on the side and woke him ... "

Acts 12:7

Evidently even the presence of an angel who
reflected the light of heaven itself wasn't enough
to wake up Peter from his sleep. No, the angel had
to strike Peter on his side to rouse him. That's a
deep sleep. No Tylenol PM. No sleeping pills. Not
even a mattress to help. Peter slept like a baby the
night before he was to be put to death, which is a
peace that is incomprehensible. Indeed, it's a peace
that only comes from the Spirit of God.

This peace, by the way, wasn't unique to St.

Peter. The Old Testament tells us that King David
was also a man who was able to sleep like a baby
even when his very life was threatened. In Psalm #3
King David wrote:

> *I lie down and sleep;*
>   *I wake again, for the Lord sustains me.*
> **I am not afraid** of ten thousands of people
>   Who have set themselves against me round
> about.

Psalm 3:5–6 RSV

What is this peace that is calm even in the threat
of death? Let me begin with what it isn't. First,
peace isn't the absence of conflict or danger. If we
had to wait for the absence of all conflict and danger before enjoying peace we would wait forever.

Abraham Lincoln was said to have had a serenity and peace about him, and yet the circumstances
that surrounded his life were anything but peace-
ful! While occupying the White House, Lincoln's
wife Mary Todd went mad and racked up thousands
of dollars of personal debt, one of his sons died
tragically, his cabinet conspired against him, his
poll popularity was in the low 40's, and his country
fought a bloody civil war. There was conflict and
danger in every area of his life. Even so, he was
still the man who was able to write the following words for his second inaugural address: "With
malice toward none, and charity for all … let us
bind up the nation's wounds." Lincoln was a man
of peace in the midst of the storm.

Peace is not the absence of conflict. It is the presence of God. This is how, when all hell is breaking loose, it is possible to be possessed of a sudden and inexplicable calm ... the kind of calm that isn't threatened by difficult circumstances, but one that thrives when circumstances are at their worst. First, Peace isn't the absence of conflict or danger.

Second, peace doesn't have much to do with our knowledge. You can possess all sorts of knowledge about peace, but that doesn't mean you are guaranteed to have it.

My wife, Stephanie and I once had the opportunity to listen to the Dali Lama speak. His message was "World Peace Through Inner Peace." One of his most interesting revelations was mentioning he knew a lot about peace and yet he still couldn't always keep his own temper with his staff. In other words, knowing about peace, and having it reign in his heart were not necessarily the same thing. Many of us are in the same boat. We know a lot about the things that make for peace, but we just don't do them. Somehow our knowledge doesn't translate to action.

Third, peace isn't always quiet. We've all heard the expression "peace and quiet." Well, silence can be just as upsetting as it is pleasant. When my four-year old son and two-year old daughter are quiet I know something is probably wrong. Peace isn't always quiet. After all, heaven isn't a particularly quiet place. It is described in Scripture as full of trumpets, singing, and shouts of praise. Indeed, there may be more silence in hell than there is in heaven. After all, Jesus described hell as the "outer darkness," and heaven as a "wedding feast," which makes hell sound like a torturous silence and heaven sound like a pretty lively place.

So then just what is peace? Well, in the Old Testament the word for peace is the Hebrew word *shalom* which means fullness or completeness. In the New Testament the word for peace is the Greek word *eirene* which means unity and harmony. Peace, therefore, can be said to be fullness and unity of heart. It is not the absence of conflict, rather it is the presence of the harmonious fullness of God.

Peace is knowing at the end of a difficult day that you're fulfilling your God-given purpose in life. Peace is when you return home to find your children safe in their beds, even if they've been fighting with each other all day. Peace is the satisfaction of knowing your career is exactly what God created you for, even if you have a difficult boss. Peace is the serenity felt when death approaches, and you know with every cell in your body that your death will lead to *more* life, not less. Peace is a good night's sleep in the hands of God as the hurricane approaches. Peace is the presence of what is good, not necessarily the absence of what is bad.

Peace tends to elude those who need to control every aspect of their lives. Control-type personalities tend to lapse into what Pastor Rick Warren calls "When and Then Thinking," which looks like this: *When* the hurricane passes and I know everything is okay, *then* I will be at peace. *When* my financial circumstances are stabilized, *then* I will be at peace. *When* my marriage gets better, *then* I will be at peace. The problem with "when and then thinking" is that it never ends. Never are the circumstances of our lives ever perfected this side of heaven! Life, by the way, isn't supposed to be perfected. It is supposed to be enjoyed ... and when that's not possible it is at least to be purposeful. Consider the lives of the apostles. Jesus promised His twelve disciples peace:

> "Peace I leave with you, my peace I give to you."
>
> *John* 14:27

And yet, in the years that followed Jesus' crucifixion and resurrection His apostles were hounded by terror everywhere. Soldiers, religious authorities, Pharisees, government officials, and spies all conspired against Jesus' disciples. They were threatened by storms, demon possessed madmen, and pennilessness. They had no homes, no job security, and no pension. Their lives were a nightmare of circumstances, and yet someone like Peter was able to sleep like a baby on the night before his trial and execution. Obviously, the peace in Peter's heart had nothing to do with the absence of conflict or danger, but with the presence of Christ.

II. How Does One Get This Peace?
The obvious question is how does one get this peace ... where does a good night's sleep come from?

The simple answer is that you don't get it, it gets you. The good news of the Gospel is that God's Spirit of peace is looking for you much harder than you are looking for it. The Spirit of God is doing everything it can to reach you. Listen to God's own assurance of His desire to give you peace:

" ... in me you may have **peace** ... "

John 16:33

Jesus is more than eager to give you peace! He is literally dying to give it to you!

Let's return to the events immediately following Jesus' death. In the three days that followed Jesus' execution His disciples had no peace. They assumed they would be murdered next by the Roman authorities. They also feared that some of Jesus' followers might seek revenge for the pathetic way they abandoned Jesus in His hour of need. Terror stalked their every thought and dream. But then the unthinkable happened. Jesus returned from the grave, found them where they hid, and said, "Peace be with you." The disciples assumed like everyone else that He was dead. But they discovered that not even death could stop Jesus from sharing His peace! When Jesus rose from the dead on Easter morning, the very first word He chose to speak to His followers was the word "peace" ...

"Peace be with you."

John 20:19

There were literally 100,000 other words Jesus could have chosen to say, such as revenge…'revenge is mine,' or repent … 'repent and return to me.' But instead He chose the word "Peace," and He literally came back from the grave to say it.

Sadly, the citizens of the post modern world look for peace in all sorts of ways: vacations to Wyoming, paying off credit card debt, and climbing the corporate ladder. The odd thing is that the harder we work for peace, the more elusive it seems to be. But the Gospel Good News is that the Peace that passes all understanding is working night and day to share itself with you. The angels of heaven will not rest until you yourself are able to rest in peace!

The night before he was tried for his life, St. Peter slept like a baby. He didn't know just what his fate would be. But this much he did know: He knew how it would all end for him … in the arms of Jesus, and He was at peace.

III. The Story of Dr. Martin Luther King
Peace At the Midnight Hour:

Perhaps no man or woman of the 20th century was stalked more ferociously than Martin Luther King. He was stabbed once. His house was bombed. Death threats upon him were more reliable than his breakfast. His phones were tapped and his living quarters were bugged by the FBI. His taxes were audited by the IRS as a matter of course. Local police monitored his every move, constantly throwing him in and out of jail. The KKK stalked him everywhere, burning crosses on his front lawn, and murdering his associates. Even members of his own Southern Christian Leadership Conference conspired against him. If any man had any right to surrender to fear it was Martin Luther King Jr. But Dr. King was a man of peace. So much so that He won the 1963 Nobel Peace Prize at the tender age of 34!

Let me share with you the account of when and how God's supernatural peace found Dr. King.

Dr. King had been a quiet and scholarly young pastor at Montgomery, Alabama's Dexter Avenue Baptist Church in 1955 when all hell broke loose. Police arrested Rosa Parks for sitting in the "whites only" section of a public bus, and the town exploded in protest. The black churches of Montgomery immediately organized a public bus boycott, and Dr. King was selected as its leader, a dangerous position in the Jim Crowe South. For the next year Dr. King and his family were subjected to an endless stream of hate letters, obscene phone calls, and death threats—as many as thirty in one day–from angry whites, local authorities, and members of the KKK. King had become the voice of the boycott, and there was nowhere in Alabama for him to hide. Living in the Church parsonage, He, his wife Coretta, and their daughter Yoki were vulnerable to any sort of attack. Reliable sources had already informed him that there were indeed assassination plots against him and his family, which scared him to death. There was no use going to the police. Most of them were conspiring against him too. Some were Klan members. The tension was withering.

One evening Dr. King returned home from a late night meeting. He collapsed into bed and tried to sleep, but then the phone rang, and when he picked up the receiver it was another ugly voice, "Nigger, if you aren't out of this town in three days we gonna blow your brains out and blow up your house." *Click*.

King paced the floor. He knew he couldn't take it anymore. The late night calls and threats—the awful fear. He went to the kitchen and poured himself a cup of coffee, and sat down at the table to brood. He knew he had to quit the bus boycott leadership for the sake of his family, and yet he knew he couldn't quit. In desperation he bowed his head into his hands and prayed out loud, "Oh Lord, I'm down here trying to do what is right. But, Lord, I must confess that I'm weak now. I'm afraid. The people are looking to me for leadership, and if I stand before them without strength and courage, they too will falter. I am at the end of my powers. I have nothing left. I can't face it alone."

Tears flowed from his eyes. But then everything changed! He suddenly felt a Presence, a stirring in himself, and discerned an inner voice speaking to him with steady assurance. "Martin Luther, stand up for righteousness. Stand up for justice. Stand up for truth. And, lo, I will be with you, even unto the end of the world." King knew it was the voice of Jesus. And the Lord continued, "I promise to never leave you, never leave you alone. No, never alone, No, never alone. I promise never to leave you, never to leave you alone … "

Martin Luther King lifted his head and felt relieved and stronger. His trembling stopped. Whatever was to happen he knew God would see it through, and he felt an inner calm he had never experienced before … the peace that the world can neither give nor take away. He knew that he could stand up without fear and face anything. He learned from this experience that God could transform "the fatigue and despair into the buoyancy of hope." He knew in his very own heart and soul the peace that passes all understanding.

At the midnight hour Dr. Martin Luther King Jr. knew without a shadow of a doubt that there was indeed peace in the storm![3]

IV. Conclusion

The time will come when you'll need God's peace. There will come a day when the circumstances of your life will come crashing down around you, and there will be no earthly reason for you to enjoy a moment's peace. As I write this message a freshman boy on one of the college campuses I serve tragically killed himself with an overdose of heroine. His parents are speechless with grief. Their midnight hour is upon them, and they are sorely in need of God's peace.

As it turns out, Jesus' disciples never found peace for themselves. What actually happened was that peace found them. When Jesus returned from the grave He gave them what they least expected—peace.

So what's in the way of peace finding you? It's incredible but true ... the peace we seek is seeking us much harder than we seek it. The Gospel Good News is that the Peace that passes all understanding is working night and day to share itself with you. The angels of heaven will not rest until you yourself are able to rest in peace!

Let me make a big shift of gears here.

Every once in a while I like to read a good "Who dunit." My favorite author for this kind of book is John Grisham. He writes novels where the good guy is always just a half step ahead of the bad guy.

Now there are two approaches to reading these kinds of books. First, you can read them the way the writer intended us to read them, from start to finish. To read them this way is to assure yourself anxiety as you read, with characters hurdling through one near death after another. The second approach to reading such books is to peek at the novel's end first, and then read the rest of the book. Peeking at the story's end eliminates anxiety, because you know how the story ends.

It is possible to peek at the end of the world's story! The New Testament describes the world's end in some detail. To peek at the end can reduce anxiety by reassuring you of one simple fact: God wins! The Bible ends with a great and conclusive battle between good and evil, where all the forces of darkness are utterly redeemed or destroyed. Much anxiety can be eliminated with the assurance that in the end the good guy wins!

How much anxiety would have been spared the world's people if at the start of World Wars I & II the Allied's victory was assured in advance? Or how much anxiety would you be spared if you knew your personal finances would eventually work out to a prosperous end! We may not know the specifics such as how much money we are going to end up with, or exactly how we will die. But we can be assured of where our eventual resting place will be, in the heart of God. This assurance of a good end is one reason why old St. Peter was able to sleep so soundly as death stalked him in that prison cell, chained to two guards. Peter slept like a baby—not because his circumstances were good, nor because he knew more about peace than the average guy. He didn't know what his fate would be the next day in his trial before King Herod. He had no idea an angel would set him free. But this much he did know; He was convinced without a shadow of a doubt how it would all end for him - in the arms of Jesus, and with that assurance He was able to sleep like a baby! Amen.

Group Study
Sleep In The Storm! (90 minutes)

Introduction (5 minutes)
Briefly:

- Offer a prize to the person who can identify each participant by name.
- Reseat yourselves and offer a 2ⁿᵈ prize to someone who can identify each participant by name.

Opening Discussion/Warm Up: (10 minutes)

Studies reveal that the average adult now sleeps two hours less each day than the average person did one hundred years ago (6.9 hrs/night vs. 9 hrs./night).

- Share how tired or rested you've generally been feeling.
- What are the culprits that conspire against you enjoying a good night's sleep (kids, TV, house work, anxiety, etc)?
- Give each participant a pencil and paper and direct them to draw a symbol for the concern that causes them the most sleeplessness.
- Show and tell.

I. What Peace Is and Isn't (15 minutes)

    a. Invite each person to share what they would do in jail on the night before their trial and execution. Ask each person to rank (1–10) how well they would sleep.

b. Read out loud Acts 12:6–7

"The very night when Herod was about to bring him out (for trial and execution), Peter was SLEEPING between two soldiers, bound with two chains ... And behold, an angel of the Lord appeared, and a light shone in the cell; and he *struck* Peter on the side and woke him ... "

Acts 12:6–7

c. Did Peter's *circumstances* justify a deep sleep ... so deep that the angel had to strike him to wake him?

d. Do you believe that Peter's *knowledge* of peace and the things that make for peace enabled him to sleep so deeply?

e. The Old Testament word for peace is the Hebrew word *shalom* which means fullness or completeness. The New Testament word for peace is the Greek word *eirene* which means unity and harmony. Using these definitions, what is the biblical understanding of "Peace?"

f. Is biblical peace the absence of trouble or the presence of God? What's the difference?

II. How Does One Get This Peace?
(15 minutes)

    a. According to the Gospel of John (John 20:19) what is the first word Jesus speaks to His disciples when He returns to them at His resurrection?

    b. Does Jesus say it once or twice (John 20:19, 21)? Is this significant?

    c. Have each participant say the word "peace" out loud in the tone they think Jesus said it to His disciples.

    d. Do you think peace is what the Disciples were expecting when they first saw Jesus?

    e. Were the disciples surprised by Jesus' greeting of "peace be with you" upon His resurrection?

    f. Based on the text of John 20:19–23 who was looking for whom the hardest— were the disciples looking for peace or was peace was looking for the disciples hardest?

    g. Share how strongly you are looking for peace. Do you believe peace is looking even more strongly for you?

III. Peace At The Midnight Hour.
(10 minutes)

    a. Based on his circumstances (stabbed once, his home bombed, countless threats, and with the KKK, FBI, IRS, local police, and even his some of his own supporters subverting him) did the Rev. Dr. Martin Luther King Jr. have any earthly reason to enjoy peace of any kind during his civil rights crusade?

b. The night before Dr. King gave his "I Have A Dream Speech" he received an assassination threat. If you had been in his shoes, would you have gone ahead and given the speech?

c. Would Dr. King say that he found peace, or that the Lord's peace found him?

IV. Conclusion (25 minutes)

a. Share a "midnight hour experience" when your world crashed in around you, and you needed peace.

b. Share what was the most helpful thing said to you during that crisis?

c. The last years of the Apostle's lives were years of hardship, suffering, and eventual death. Did these disciples have any earthly reason to enjoy a good night's sleep?

d. Read out loud together from Psalm 3:5–6
I lie down and SLEEP;
   I wake again, for the Lord sustains me.
I am not afraid of ten thousands of people
   Who have set themselves against me
   round about.

e. What might stop you from receiving this peace?

Warm Up (10 minutes)

a. Share your prayer requests, and update one another on any progress.

b. Confirm the time and locations of the next group study.

c. Close by reading together the following prayer.

Dear God,

You are fully aware of every detail of my life's circumstances. Indeed, You not only know my past and present, but You know everything about my future. I pray, Lord, that I would rest in You ... that I would trust that no matter what happens in my life that I can rest in the confidence that my life will end up in Your arms. Amen.

CHAPTER FOUR:
PATIENCE

Hurry Is Not Of The Devil,
Hurry Is The Devil!

What is the first word you would choose to describe love? Movies and television would lead you to think of the word "passion." Politically correct psycho-babble links love with "tolerance." Books on marriage focus on love as "commitment." But God Himself chose a different word. Of the 60,000 common words in English that could have been used, the first word God chose to describe love was *patience*. He begins His definition of love by saying:

"Love is patient ... "

1 Corinthians 13:4

It's not a sexy definition, neither is it trendy, but "patience" is God's first word for defining love. In other words, God says that before passion, tolerance, and commitment, love is first of all, patient.

This is why mothers and fathers the world over tell their 18-year old daughters again and again, "If he really loves you, he'll wait."

It's also why parents the world over learn the age-old wisdom in raising their children, love is spelled T-I-M-E.

The Old Testament offers an exquisite story that crystallizes the relationship between love and patience. It is found in Genesis and the story of Jacob's love for Rachel. Genesis tells us that Jacob was in search of a wife, and when he first laid eyes on Rachel he was struck breathless. So smitten with love was he that tears just ran down his face. It took Jacob only a few days to ask Rachel's father Laban for her hand in marriage, but her father was a crafty old coot, and greedy too. Laban knew just how smitten and vulnerable Jacob was, and how to take advantage of the situation. So Laban offered Rachel to Jacob, BUT with the condition that he first serve as the family shepherd for seven years. Naturally, Jacob agreed to the bargain, for he would have done anything to win Rachel's hand. Genesis tells us that the seven years of service passed quickly for Jacob, for as the Scripture says, " *... they seemed to him but a few days because of the love he had for her*" (Genesis 29:20).

True love empowers the heart with the determination to wait as long as necessary. Love's DNA has written into it the wisdom, "All good things come to those who wait."

Love and patience are two sides of the same coin. If you love to garden, you'll be patient enough to wait for your seeds to sprout. If you love music, you'll be patient as you learn to play the instrument of your choice. If you love your husband or wife, you will be patient with their quirks and faults.

Sadly, this relationship between love and patience has been turned upside down by popular culture, which insists that love means to speed up rather than slow down. Love today is all about immediate gratification. Newly released movies tell us that falling in love means to rush into sexual intimacy. But this isn't the way God made His world. From the very beginning God wove an intimate connection between love and patience. At the very center of love's mystery is understanding that patience is the surest evidence of love's presence.

So ... if you've ever wondered whether or not someone loves you, wonder no more. Rest assured that wherever there is love there is patience. One does not exist without the other.

Of course, few have the patience they feel they need, especially in marriage. This is illustrated by the following fable from Africa:

A tribal woman had become increasingly impatient with her husband, causing a strain in their marriage. She was forever blowing up at him, and she knew this wasn't right, so she went to her local medicine man to get help. He told her that she must first gather the basic ingredients for such a powerful medicine. The first thing he needed was three hairs from the mane of a live lion. The lady left the doctor wondering how in the world she was going to get close enough to a lion to get three hairs. She decided to take her largest goat and tie it to a tree, hoping to tempt the lion. Sure enough, the lion came and took the goat. The next day she tied another goat to the tree, and the process went on for several weeks until she had sacrificed her entire flock as bait. Each day she managed to get closer to the lion and on the final day managed to talk to him. "I'm sorry to trouble you, but I wonder if I could have three hairs from your mane?"

The lion smiled and said, "Of course, take what you wish. After all, I've enjoyed your goats."

The next day the woman triumphantly took the ingredients to the medicine man. The doctor turned to her and said, "You must have been extremely patient to get these hairs from the mane of a live lion. Now go home and put the same amount of patience into your marriage, and you'll be fine!"

Like I said, few feel as if they have the patience they need. Most folks fall into the category illustrated by the old bumper sticker: *"I need patience … and I need it right NOW!!!"* After all, Americans do just about anything but wait. We won't wait for food—it's a fast food culture. We don't wait for money—credit cards enable us to spend it before we earn it. We don't wait for God; we're much too busy to pray. Rather than seeing patience as an essential expression of love, we view it as a luxury we don't have time for. Unfortunately hurry is spiritually corrosive. When we hurry we are too busy for the things of God, which is why the great Christian psychiatrist Carl Jung wrote:

"Hurry is not of the devil; Hurry is the devil."

Think about it: how much trouble has your hurry gotten you into with your family, your work, and your neglected friends? And how much has your hurried lifestyle kept you from God? Being in a hurry sounds innocent enough. After all, there is nothing immoral about being in a hurry. *But* hurry rarely gets us to where we want to go ... especially with God. Indeed, hurry is a modern enemy of spiritual health. It is a spiritual cancer that grows unnoticed in our hearts till the day we no longer have time for God.

With this chapter I will share a simple principle—God Himself never hurries. Because He never hurries it is His intention to help you escape the treadmill of a frantic pace. The rat race is meant for rats! So in the next couple of pages I'll share some of God's wisdom that will help you escape the rat race and rejoin the human race. You won't even have to pluck any hair from a lion's mane!

I. God Doesn't Hurry!
It's healthy to keep in mind that God doesn't hurry. Just because we're in a hurry, doesn't mean God is. There is an old Negro spiritual that says, "God is

never late, He's never early, He's always right on time." It's true. God's timing is perfect.

But if God doesn't hurry we live in a frantic culture that hardly slows down enough to enjoy a family meal together. Even our spiritual lives seem to add to the rush. Take church attendance for example. Too often the church makes its member's lives all the busier. To crowded family schedules a church can add weekly worship, meetings, conferences, groups, special meals, studies, and all sorts of service projects. One of the damnable things organized religion does is get its followers busy for God. The devil, in turn, can use all this hurry to manipulate mischief. Hurried people are tired, short tempered, and quarrelsome ... a perfect mix for upsets. The pace of our American lifestyle, even in church, conspires against taking the time for the kind of meaningful relationships that feed our souls and nourish our spirits.

But it's not simply our fast paced culture that's to blame. Not only does patience run counter to our culture, but it also runs against the grain of our human nature. My four-year old son Jackson doesn't wait for anything. He runs everywhere, from pillar to post all day. If he can't enjoy something immediately he'll raise his arms and run around the room screaming, and then he'll go find something else to do. We are not patient beings by nature, and the devil takes terrible advantage of this character flaw. Some of his best work is achieved when people are too busy for their own good. As the old saying goes:

> "If the devil can't make you bad, he'll make you busy."

So let me ask you a question. Just how busy are you? If you're too busy to take time with God, if you're too busy to enjoy meaningful time with your family, and if you're too hurried to stop and help a friend, then you're too busy. You see, one of the biggest problems we all face in life is that we get so busy that we neglect the things that are most important. We don't do this intentionally … we simply get in a hurry.

In Jesus' famous story of the Good Samaritan, a man traveling on the road from Jerusalem to Jericho is attacked by robbers, beaten, and left for dead along the side of the road. A short time later a priest passes by and does nothing. Why? Probably because he felt too busy. Being an important man, he may have assumed that someone else would pass by who had more time to attend to the needs of the wounded man. A second man came by, but he too did nothing but pass by, and no doubt he justified his inaction because of all his other obligations. Again, as Jesus' story illustrates, the devil doesn't have to make us bad. He only has to make us feel too busy to do those things we think are most important.

This isn't just soft hearted, sentimental idealism. Our hurry exacts huge financial costs. I read recently that the annual cost of drivers running red lights in medical bills and car repairs alone is 7 billion dollars annually. All this to save an average of 50 seconds per stop light. And if it is expensive to run a red light, it is infinitely more expensive to ignore God's warning signs. When God tells us to slow down and we ignore His warning, there is always hell to pay.

Let me to share a second spiritual principle:

"To lift you up, God will slow you down."

I hate going slow, and I have the speeding tickets to prove it. But the problem is that the Christian life is all about following God, and God doesn't hurry. God didn't hurry when He created the world. He took six days to make it when He could have done it all at once. Evidently He wanted to take His time and enjoy the process. And after creating the universe God certainly had a lot to do, but He didn't hurry. Instead, he took the seventh day off.

The best illustration to confirm that God doesn't hurry is this: There isn't one passage in the New Testament that describes Jesus running.

There are descriptions of Him resting, waiting, walking, and stopping ... but not one of Jesus running. Evidently He didn't hurry. And this of course is one of the great frustrations of following Jesus. We want Him to go faster.

We pray, and expect an immediate answer. A family member gets sick, and we demand an instantaneous healing. We share the Gospel with an unbelieving friend, and we expect a spontaneous conversion. We expect God to hurry and do our bidding, but He doesn't work that way. He walks where He goes even when we expect Him to run.

The Bible tells the strange story of how Jesus wouldn't even hurry when asked to visit a dear friend's death bed. The story is in John, chapter 11. In this account, Jesus is told that His good friend Lazarus is near death. But rather than rush to Lazarus' side, the Bible reports that Jesus intentionally ...

> " ... stayed two days longer in the place where He was."
>
> *John* 11:6

Why did Jesus wait? Why wouldn't He hurry to Lazarus' sick bed? Indeed, Jesus never did make it until four days after Lazarus' death, and his family and friends were upset. They had sent messages telling of Lazarus' illness, but rather than hurry, Jesus waited. Both of Lazarus' sisters questioned Jesus' loyalty when he finally arrived. They said accusingly, "Lord, if you had been here, my brother would not have died" (John 11:21). Fortunately, the Lord was patient. He knew they couldn't understand the purpose for His waiting—that He intended to do something much greater than what they wanted. Lazarus' family and friends wanted their brother to be healed, but Jesus was preparing a resurrection.

This same scenario is played out in our own lives. A family member gets sick, we pray for Jesus' help, but nothing happens. He does not hurry but waits, which drives us crazy ... and often we then take matters into our own hands. But if it is difficult to wait for God, it is that much harder to wish you had.

Fortunately, the Lord is ever patient, even when we grow impatient with Him. He knows we don't understand how much more He wants to do than what we are asking for. He knows we don't fully comprehend His promise:

> God " ... is able to do far more than we would ever dare to ask or even dream of ... "

Ephesians 3:20

We tend to pray for small things, while God prepares big things. We pray for earthly concerns, while he prepares us for heaven. We look for prayers to be answered immediately, while God concerns Himself with forever. Our ways are not God's ways, and so we grow impatient with a God who never hurries. Fortunately, God is patient with our impulses and urgency. He chooses to respond carefully and deliberately. We may be victims of the urgent, but He never is.

II. How Do You Get Patience?

So the obvious question is how does one acquire the kind of patience that helps us slow down our hurried life-style? The Bible prescribes two specific ways for developing patience. The first was written by Jesus' brother James:

> "Count it all joy, my brethren, when you meet various trials, for you know that the testing of your faith produces *patience* ... " (James 1:2–3).

The Greek word for patience used here is the word *macrothumia*. *Macro* means long and *thumia* means temper. So the word literally means 'long temper,' and it suggests that going through hard times can give one a long temper ... just the opposite of a short fuse. Said more simply, hard times soften our hearts with patience.

During a summer vacation Stephanie and I were in Washington D.C. where we visited the newly opened Franklin D. Roosevelt memorial. At the entrance to the memorial there was a huge sculpture of President Roosevelt in his wheelchair. Somewhere in the exhibit I read a quote from his wife Eleanor who remarked that her husband became a much better and more patient man after having been struck down by polio. In other words, his patience was lifted up after he had been struck down.

Hard times bring out the best in people. The English word "patience" comes from the Latin word *pati* which means "to endure," and it also comes from the Greek word *pathos* which means "to suffer." Patience quite literally means to endure suffering. The way to learn patience is to go through hard times.

The story is told about a young Christian who went to an old believer for some prayer because he wanted to become more patient. They knelt down together and the old man began to pray, "Lord, send this young man tribulation for breakfast, problems for lunch, and suffering for supper."[14]

Our patience grows up when the hard times come down!

The second way the Bible prescribes patience is by taking hold of hope. The Bible says:

> "Now hope that is seen is not hope. For who hopes for what he sees? But if we hope for what we do not see, we wait for it with *patience*."
>
> *Romans* 8:24–25

I spent 20 years as a young man hoping to get married. My first prayer for a wife came when I was 22 years old, but I didn't marry Stephanie till I was 42. It was a long 20 year wait to be sure, but what gave me patience was the hope that God had someone special just for me. If an angel had told me at 22 that I would have to wait for 20 years before being married, I don't know I would have made it. Instead, God was merciful, and made me wait only one day at a time, and along the way I became a more patient person. I was able to wait because God gave me the hope that He had someone special picked just for me, and He did!

Patience comes when we hope for what we do not see.

III. The Lord Is Patient With You!

Whenever I feel impatient it helps me to consider how patient God is with me. The Bible says:

"God is patient with you."

2 Peter 3:9

When I'm tempted with impatience it's helpful to keep in mind God's patience with me. It provides a larger perspective. Here I am reminded of a story of how one's man's impatience was utterly transformed with the help of a larger perspective.

A train was filled with tired people who had spent the day traveling through the hot dusty plains and were at last settling down for a good night's sleep. However, at one end of the car a man was holding a tiny baby who became restless and started screaming at the top of its lungs. Unable to take it any longer, a big brawny man spoke for the rest of the group. "Why don't you take that baby to its mother?" There was a moment's pause and then came the reply. "I'm sorry. I'm doin' my best. The baby's mother is in a casket in the baggage car in front of us." There was an awkward silence for a couple minutes. Then the same man who asked the cruel question got out of his seat and moved toward the father of the motherless child. He apologized for his impatience. He took the tiny baby in his own arms and told the tired father to get some sleep. He then patiently cared for the little baby all through the night.

God is patient with us because He has a much larger perspective–He sees what the human eye can't. He sees our past, present, and future all at once, taking it all into His heart in our behalf.

God is patient! And when His Spirit is planted in us we develop a larger perspective—ever more able to look at others from God's perspective. In so doing our capacity for patience is charged with a supernatural empathy, the simple result being that we become more patient.

IV. What Does God's Patience Look Like?

So what does God's patience look like?

Well it can be described with such synonyms as tolerance, endurance, poise, perseverance, diligence and constancy. It was embodied by old Job himself who weathered the devil's worst, yet managed to keep his heart open to God. It was at the center of Christ's character, who willingly endured mankind's worst so that He could give each of us His best. Patience was evident in St. Paul's persistence, John Wesley's endurance, and Mother Teresa of Calcutta's resilience. These are all awesome examples. But I will always remember what God's patience looked like when it first showed itself to me personally.

The first church I ever served as pastor was a little country church in the village of Roseville, Pennsylvania. It was a town with more cows than people, but every Sunday morning 73 saints gathered for worship. These people didn't come to worship because I had anything helpful or uplifting to say. They knew from the moment they first laid eyes on me that I was green as grass, and didn't know a thing. Even so, they concluded it was their responsibility to teach me how to be a pastor, which required God-inspired patience on their part 'cause I honestly had no idea what I was doing.

I remember well the day I messed up the wedding of the Lay Leader's daughter. I pulled into my driveway on her wedding day at 1:30 in the afternoon, and went inside for some lemonade before scooting over to the Church for the 2 p.m. wedding. I flopped onto my couch for a quick look through the paper when my front door burst open and the bride's cousin looked down at me in disbelief.

"Win, what are you doin'?" Blurted Travis.

"Relax, Travis; we have 25 minutes 'till the wedding."

"Win, the wedding was at 1pm!"

I jumped out of the couch fully expecting to catch an earful from the bride and her father. I could see them both standing in the hot sun as I ran to the Church, she in her wedding gown and her dad in his blue suit. I could hear the organist inside playing through her 17th rendition of *Here Comes the Bride*. It was September 1st, and there was no air conditioning. Everyone inside was frantically fanning themselves. They all had every reason for lost patience, especially the bride and her father. But when I reached the Church the father reached out his hand, grabbed mine and said warmly, "Win, we love you. Let's get started."

Wow!

It was no human patience the bride's father bestowed upon me. It was a divinely inspired patience ... a fruit of God's spirit.

Jesus' followers experienced many such moments of supernatural patience. Time and time again His disciples made mistakes, and every time Jesus would patiently use their mistakes to teach His love. For Christ, mistakes were the best opportunities to learn. Even during His own crucifixion Jesus patiently taught those willing to learn. The easiest way to begin growing in patience is simply to let Him love you. Like I said, love and patience are two sides of the same coin. When you open your heart to His love your hard times will be transformed into divinely inspired patience.

This was certainly the experience of Adoniram and Ana Judson, America's first foreign missionaries, who patiently endured harrowing tribulations in Burma for the sake of sharing the love of Christ.

V. The Story of Adoniram & Ann Judson: America's First Foreign Missionaries

On February 5th, 1812 Adoniram Judson married Ann Haseltine in Salem, Massachusetts. Fourteen days later they set sail for India as America's first foreign missionaries. Their four month voyage was trying, but their trials at sea proved only the beginning of their hardship. First, they were denied entrance to Calcutta by the British East India Company who did not want any of their trade endangered by Christians sharing the Gospel with Hindus. They tried to land at Madras, but were again rejected and threatened with deportation. Somehow a door opened for them in Rangoon, Burma. Their passage on the Sea of

Bengal was storm-tossed by a monsoon and Ann was struck deathly ill. Even so, she somehow managed to deliver their first child, who died at birth, and was buried at sea. Grief stricken, sick, fearful, and alone, the Judsons arrived in Rangoon, a foul and filthy village full of darkness, corruption, and danger. They didn't speak the language, know the culture, nor were there any Christians to welcome and support them in this country of millions. As they prayed in their ship before going ashore they anguished themselves with the thought that a speedy death from disease or at the hands of cruel officials might be the best fate for which they could hope. But in their prayer they sensed the Lord reassuring them, "Fear not," He said, "for I am with thee; be not dismayed for I am thy God." Ann was so sick she had to disembark from the ship on a stretcher, but somehow they managed to survive.

It was six soul-crushing years before they won their first convert to Christ. Soon thereafter Adoniram was arrested. He was accused of being a British spy and condemned to death. Ann's prayers and tireless efforts pleading with officials spared his life. His imprisonment lasted 21 months, where he was locked with many others in a windowless chamber chained to stocks and fed only occasionally. The filth and stench of his cell was not even fit for animals. Miraculously, Adoniram survived, and was eventually released through British intervention. He returned to his house only to find his wife and child all but starved to death. The trials just kept coming. Yet through it all this man and woman of faith not only won many to Christ, but they also mastered the Burmese language, translated the Bible into Burmese, and wrote the definitive Burmese/English dictionary. Their resolve, born through inhuman affliction, served to enlarge their hearts to a superhuman patience!

At the time of Adoniram's death in 1850, after thirty eight years of patient ministry, a Burmese government survey recorded 210,000 Christians, one out of every sixty Burmese. Today 6% of the Burmese (Myanmar) population is Christian, a testimony to the patient resolve of two faithful disciples of Christ.

I can't say for sure what word Adoniram and Ann Judson would use to describe love. I do know what word comes to my mind in light of their history—*patience*!

As the Scripture declares: "Love is patient!"

Group Study:
Hurry Is Not Of The Devil,
Hurry Is The Devil! (90 minutes)

Introduction (5 minutes)
Briefly:

- Identify the participant who has received the most speeding tickets over the past three years.
- Identify the participant who has eaten the fewest meals at home in the past week.
- Identify participants who feel they must hurry through their day-to-day life. Share examples.

Opening Discussion/Warm Up: (10 minutes)

- What is the first word that comes to your mind to define "love"? What is the first word St. Paul uses (1 Corinthians 13:4) to define love? What are some of the biblical stories you can think of that link love with patience? List them. Can you think of any contemporary news stories that link love with patience? Share them.
- What did Carl Jung mean when he wrote, "Hurry is not of the devil, hurry is the devil." Share examples from your life.

I. God Doesn't Hurry (20 minutes)
   a. If God doesn't hurry does that mean that

God is out of step with a frenzied 21st century North American culture?

b. Can you identify a single passage in the New Testament where Jesus is running or in a hurry?

c. How does the devil use our busyness against us?

d. What does the phrase, "If the devil can't make you bad, he'll make your busy" mean?

e. In Jesus' story of the Good Samaritan (Luke 10:29–37) were the priest and Levite uncaring, or were they just too busy to help?

f. Share an occasion when you were too busy to help someone in need.

g. When God seems slow to act, what are the possibilities?

    i. He doesn't hear our prayers.

    ii. He doesn't care.

    iii. He doesn't have the power/ authority to help.

    iv. He is too busy Himself.

    v. He is preparing something better than what we want/expect/hope.

II. How Do You Get Patience? (10 minutes)

a. According to James 1:2–3 how does one get patience?

"Count it all joy, my brethren, when you meet various trials, for you know

that the testing of your faith produces
patience ... "

James 1:2–3

"Patience" comes from the Latin word
pati which means "to endure," and it
also comes from the Greek word *pathos*
which means "to suffer." Patience quite
literally means to endure suffering.

b. According to Romans 8 how do you get
patience?

"Now hope that is seen is not hope. For
who hopes for what he sees? But if we
hope for what we do not see, we wait for
it with *patience*"

Romans 8:24–25

Patience comes when we hope for what we do not see.

III. The Lord is Patient With Us (10 minutes)

a. Read 2 Peter 3:9 - "God is patient with
you."
b. Have each participant share the occasion when they came to believe God was
patient with them.

IV. What Does God's Patience Look Like (10 minutes)

a. Read out loud the story of Jesus raising
Lazarus (Luke 11:1–44).
b. Why did Jesus wait two extra days (Luke
11:6) after hearing that Lazarus was sick?

     c. Does Jesus' two day wait seem like patience or uncaring to the sisters of Lazarus (John 11:21, 32)?

     d. Does Jesus do what everyone wanted Him to do at the beginning of the story? Does He do something better instead?

V. The Story of Adoniram and Ann Judson (15 minutes)

     a. Have someone read the Judsons story from the text of this chapter.

     b. From the description of their lives, does it sound like the Judson's possessed a superhuman patience?

     c. How similar was their patience with that of Jesus?

     d. Does Jesus promise to strengthen your patience, or to give you a wholly new/ supernatural patience via His Holy Spirit? (Galatians 5:22)

Warm Up: (5 minutes)

     a. Share prayer requests within the group

     b. Confirm the time and location of the next group study

     c. Close by reading out loud the following prayer:

Dear God,

We live in a frantic / fast paced culture, but You live in forever. Our two worlds are not the same, and we constantly want You to adjust Your time-table to our own. We want You to hurry up. We want You to join our frenzy. But that of course is not the way You work. It is not You who is to conform to us, but we who are to conform to You—to Your ways, to Your life, and to Your timetable. Help us Lord to let go of the tyranny of today, and give us Your perspective of forever. Help us to measure the importance and urgency of things by their place in heaven as opposed to their place in the here and now. Help us Lord, to live in the forever right now! Amen.

CHAPTER FIVE:
KINDNESS

Kindness That Works!

I'm one of those individuals who likes to be on time for the start of a Major League Baseball game. It's a personal fetish of mine. Before the first pitch is thrown I like to be in my seat, with a hot dog and fries on my lap, my drink in the cup holder, my hat on, and the sun block applied. So I was a bit edgy when I arrived behind schedule for a Florida Marlins game. My friend Spencer and I, along with our two boys, arrived at 6:54p.m., just barely enough time to find our seats for the 7:05 start. As you might imagine, I was hurrying us along. In haste I thought the elevator our most efficient means up to the 200 level. But when the elevator door opened we hesitated as an elderly blind man carefully stepped out with his walking

stick. Now you don't see many blind men at baseball games, so we waited patiently and then hurried aboard. But just as the elevator doors were
shutting, my pal Spencer suddenly slipped out with
the parting words, "Take the kids; I'll meet you at
the seats."

Well, I made it on time for the first pitch. And about
eighteen minutes later Spencer rejoined us. Naturally, I
was curious where he had gone, so he shared the following reflection.

"The elderly gentleman getting out of that elevator was indeed totally blind but he had no help,
and I was concerned he might have a tough time
fighting his way through the crowd, so I decided to
be useful. He showed me his ticket and together we
navigated through the hoards of people and picked
our way down the stairs to his seat. Once there we
got to talking, so I sat with him for a while. He
shared that even though he was blind, still he liked
baseball, and particularly liked going to the game
to smell the beer and popcorn, to feel the excite-
ment, and to hear the crack of the bat and the roar
of the crowd while following the game's progress
on his portable radio."

Before leaving Spencer shared an encouraging
word and offered his cell number in case the gentleman could use some assistance during or after
the game. It was just like my friend Spencer, to be
kind by being useful.

In today's world we need all the kindness we can
give and get. Let's face it, kindness is easily lost or over-

looked in our competitive 21st century culture. Our "survival of the fittest" mentality divides the winners from the losers, the beautiful from the homely, the smart from the dull, and the rich from the poor. We watch football games to enjoy the "big hit," hockey games for the gloves-off fight, and boxing matches for the knock out punch. *Fortune Magazine* lists the 100 wealthiest. *People Magazine* lists the best and worst dressed. And the Wall Street Journal keeps a stead eye on who's up and who's down in the business world. Our American culture is not kind to the losers of all this competition, which is precisely why kindness is so life-giving in our "dog eat dog" world.

I. Kindness is Useful

The fifth of the nine fruit of the Spirit listed by St. Paul in Galatians 5:22 is kindness. Unfortunately the English word "kindness" does not capture the fullness of the Scripture's original meaning when St. Paul lists it as the 5th of the nine fruits. The precise Greek word employed is *crestotes*, a word which suggests "usefulness" and "employment." In other words, St. Paul's intended meaning for "kindness" is one that is inclined to usefulness. It is not a word that simply communicates sentiment or compassion, but one that emphasizes utility. According to St. Paul kindness is best expressed when you are useful. We all know people who are quite friendly, but who aren't particularly useful just as we know some religious folk who are so heavenly minded they are no earthly good. But when St. Paul writes of kindness he has in mind a very practical character trait, one that tangibly benefits others for their own sake.

Here, I must confess that I have a personal bias about the word kindness. I think our current use of it in America is too soft, if not a bit sappy. To be described as "kind" in today's competitive world can be a bit limp; it's warm and friendly, but not particularly dynamic. By contrast St. Paul employs the robust Greek word *crestotes* for kindness which is all about an excellence of character that inspires one to tangible and practical usefulness. This definition taps into a deep root of Christian theology which is most profoundly expressed in the Bible's Letter of James. James 2:20 famously states:

"Faith without works is dead."

James 2:20

In other words our well-being and our well-doing are connected, and according to the language of scripture God measures kindness more by what we *do* than by any warmth or sympathy we may communicate. As the Letter of James states:

"If a brother or sister is ill clad and in lack of daily food, and one of you says to them, "Go in peace, be warmed and filled," without giving them the things needed for the body, what does it profit? So faith by itself, if it has no works, is dead."

James 2:15–17

James' message above captures the sprit of kindness as St. Paul references it. Kindness is all about doing the work of love. Indeed, verse 17 could be rephrased to say 'kindness without usefulness is dead.' It's not enough to feel compassion to express kindness. The kindness that grows out of God's spirit does the work of love for the sake of others.

My wife Stephanie and I have three small children, and we're raising them to have an ambition for kindness. John Wesley defined this ambition when he wrote:

> "Do all the good you can. By all the means you
> can. In all the ways you can. In all the places
> you can. At all the times you can. To all the
> people you can. As long as ever you can."

Not only does this kindness reflect the spirit of God, but I've also noticed that genuinely useful people are usually well-stocked with friends and funds. They're popular because they are all about adding value to others. As Zig Ziegler used to say, "If you spend your life helping others with what they need, you will always have what you need."

Kindness is contagious. It seems that the more kindness you share, the more kindness comes back to bless you.

But even when you aren't feeling particularly kind, the good news of the Gospel is that God is ready, willing, and able to shower you with the kindness you may not be willing or able to share. It's never a question of whether God is willing to supply such kindness, the only question is whether or not you are willing to accept God's kindness on His terms.

II. What Does Kindness Look Like To God?

So what exactly does kindness look like to God? Is it letting someone go ahead of you in traffic, or picking up the garbage from your neighbor's fallen trash can? What is kindness on God's terms? You get an idea of just how radical it is in Jesus' "Sermon on the Plain." In this sermon Jesus establishes a clear standard for God's kindness. He says:

> " ... love your enemies, and do good, and lend, expecting nothing in return ... for (God) is *kind* to the ungrateful and the selfish."

> *Luke 6:35*

What does God's kindness look like? According to Jesus God's kindness is all about loving enemies, lending with no expectation of return, and being kind to the ungrateful and the selfish. This is no human standard! Jesus isn't just telling you to love your friends and treat them nicely, nor is He suggesting that you merely put up with rude people and do your best not to lose your temper with those who are selfish and self-centered. No, Jesus is much more radical, taking you far beyond the boundary of decency and civility.

What does kindness look like to God? Jesus goes on to describe it vividly with His most famous story of all–the story of the Good Samaritan.

An Israelite man was walking from Jerusalem to Jericho when he fell into the hands of bandits, who robbed him, beat him, and left him along the side of the road half dead. A priest traveling that same road came upon him, but when he saw the man's wounds he passed by, not wanting to get involved. Likewise a deacon passed by, but he was afraid he would be late for his appointment if he stopped to lend aid. Then a Samaritan, an avowed enemy of every Jew, came upon the wounded man. This Samaritan had compassion for the Israelite, AND HE DID SOMETHING ABOUT IT! He tended to the Jew and nursed him. He then took him to safety and spent his own money to secure him care. He did so, not because he liked the Jew. He didn't know him. He stopped and helped because God's Spirit inspired him to go beyond the limits of his own heart to show kindness.

This is Jesus' story of kindness, and it describes a response beyond any human standard for moral decency. First, the Jews and Samaritans were natural enemies. In Jesus' day Jews and Samaritans had hated each other for centuries, so the Samaritan had to somehow get past his prejudice to help. Second, the Samaritan needed to be willing to lend without any expectation of return. The money he spent would not be coming back to him. Third, the Samaritan may well have had to be kind to someone who would be ungrateful. There would be no hearty thanks and recognition for his efforts. He would have to be kind to the Jew on God's terms alone.

As I've said, such kindness is far beyond any human standard, and one that frankly has no realistic expectation of fulfillment by any normal man or woman. After all, it's hard enough being kind to individuals you love, let alone to the ungrateful and selfish. Simply put, God's standard for kindness is way beyond any human capacity.

Fortunately God doesn't expect you to fulfill His standard yourself. Indeed, quite the opposite. He expects you to lay yourself aside. Because kindness on God's terms is beyond anything you could ever possibly achieve. It's not supposed to be your achievement. It's God's work. It's all about God taking over the controls of your heart, mind, soul and body so that it is no longer you who are doing it, but Christ who lives within you. Living on God's terms is nothing more than the ancient Christian creed of dying to self that Christ might live within. It's not living for Christ, but living in Him.

By the way, when you actually do this—when you welcome His Lordship over your life, you can experience for yourself the wonder of what St. Paul described:

> "I can do all things through Christ who strengthens me."
>
> *Philippians* 4:13

You will astound yourself by being kind to even the most despicable of people.

I hasten to add that God is no hypocrite. He is unfailingly kind, maintaining His own standard of kindness. God is useful to the righteous as well as to the unrighteous. He does not discriminate. He does not treat His enemies any differently than He does His friends. As the Scripture affirms:

> "He causes His sun to rise on the evil and the good, and sends rain on the righteous and the unrighteous."
>
> *Matthew* 5:45

God is unfailingly kind, and His kindness is as practical and tangible as a warm summer rain on a parched July day.

I know of no better story of an individual whose kindness was lived out on God's terms than Ida Scudder, a 20th century medical missionary to India. In 1894 her college ambition was to marry a millionaire husband. But God touched her heart through the sufferings of the people she loved in India, and within her grew an entirely new ambition: the simple goal of being useful.

III. The Story of Ida Scudder:[13]

Ida Scudder did not want to become a missionary. Never! India was too hot, too dusty and too over-crowded—with most of the seething masses dirty or destitute; leprous or lice-ridden. Besides, a missionary bungalow was no place for a blossoming young lady (fresh out of college) with dreams of debutante balls and beaus, dresses and dances, and eventual marriage to a millionaire. Neither would the expectation generated by the "Scudder family tradition" sway her.

- What if her grandfather John was America's first foreign medical missionary?!

- What if all his sons followed in his footsteps?

- What if all the other grandchildren were planning on doing the same?

Not *Ida*! S*he* would not be forced into the Scudder family mold. She had only returned to India to nurse her ailing mother back to health, then it was back to the good life in America. That much was certain! Or so she thought until it all suddenly changed one terrible night. Ida was up late in her bungalow reading, when she was interrupted by a knock. It was a high cast Brahmin:

"Ammal! I desperately need your help. My wife, a young girl of only 14, is dying in childbirth."

"Oh!" exclaimed Ida in swift sympathy. "It's my father you want. He's the doctor. He's right next door. I'll take you to him."

"What!" exclaimed the Brahmin in haughty outrage. "Permit a man to look upon my wife?! It is better that she should die!"

Ida was aghast.

"There's nothing you can do," explained her father. "It's the custom. It would violate his caste law."

Shaking, she returned to her book. Then again,

footsteps sounded on the veranda. This time, a Mohammedan:

"Salaam, Madam. May Allah give you peace. If you could help me. It's my wife. The child will not come. I am afraid she is dying … "

Ida gasped, "My father will help, he's … "

"Madam," the voice was apologetic but firm, "You don't understand our ways. Only men of the immediate family enter a Moslem woman's room. It is you, a *woman*, whose help I seek. Not a man's."

"But I can't help," sputtered Ida, "I'm not even a nurse."

"Then my wife must die," returned the Moslem in stolid resignation. "It is the will of Allah."

Ida was left with her book, but could not read. She lay awake on her bed. It was then the third knock came. To her horror, another with the same plea. He, too, had a young wife dying in labor. Would Ida come?

"Don't you understand? There's nothing I can do."

"I could not sleep that night—it was too terrible," Ida later recalled. "Here … were 3 young girls dying because there was no woman to help them. I spent the night in anguish and prayer … I think that was the first time I ever met God face-to-face." With the first light came the beating of the 'tom-toms'—the death message—for all 3 girls had died that night. Ida remained in her room wrestling with God. When she finally emerged, she found her father and mother and resolutely announced:

"I'm going to America to study to be a doctor

so I can come back here and help the women of India."

That's just what Ida did. Cornell Medical College had opened its doors to women and Ida was enrolled with the first class (class of 1899). Ida not only graduated, but while in America she also raised over $10,000 to build a new hospital for India. November 22, 1899, Ida set sail. It was a challenging start. Her father, from whom she expected to receive her residency died just months after her return. Her first patient died, as did the next. But her healing skills were soon confirmed and the veranda of her 8' by 10' room was crowded from dawn to dusk.

In the years to come Ida's growing kindness added the teaching of medical students and taking in orphans onto her responsibilities.

And it was not just kindness her patients received, it was genuine Christian love. Few of her patients escaped without learning something of her love for God. Once a Mohammedan woman, recovering from a sudden attack of acute malarial mania, seized Ida's hand. "Tell me, why did you not lose your temper with me when I went out of my mind?" Before Ida could answer, a Hindu woman in the next bed responded:

"Don't you know why? That's what their God is like, 'long-suffering and slow to anger.'"

On her 88th birthday, Cornell University Medical College conferred upon Ida—their first female graduate - its highest honor: "The Award of Distinction." Her work had grown beyond her wildest imagination. The one bed for healing in her father's mission bungalow had now become more than 1,000. The first class of 14 medical students had swelled to 900 each year. And her staff had multiplied to include 380 doctors, 400 nurses and 270 paramedical workers serving nearly 2,500 patients in a single day.

Ida Scudder could be described with many words—faithful, heroic, compassionate, brave and steadfast, to name a few. But the most precise word might just be "kind." Ida's faith in Christ and her love for the suffering women of India inspired her to lay aside her own dreams for the sake of being useful to the sick, the orphan, and to those who wanted to serve God through medicine. Ida's kindness was expressed practically and tangibly through her ministry to those who needed help! Certainly, she is a sterling example of how "You can do all things through Christ who strengthens you." Ida accepted God's kindness on His terms and by His Spirit helped transform India's health care during the 20th century, all by answering the call to be useful. Steven Grellet, a French Quaker, once wrote words that well express the kindness of Ida's life:

> "I shall pass through this world but once. Any good I can do, or any *kindness* that I can show any human being, let me do it now and not defer it. For I shall not pass this way again."

Ida Scudder did not waste her opportunity to extend kindness to those she served. And God can accomplish equal wonders through you when you accept His kindness on His terms. You will become one who loves your enemies, does them good, lends without expectation of return, and who is useful to the ungrateful and the selfish. It's a worthy ambition!

Group Study:
Kindness That Works! (90 minutes)

Introduction (15 minutes)
Briefly:
- Share with a partner (one on one) an instance when someone was kind to you for no reason. How did it make you feel? What did it look like to you? How did you feel before, during, and after the experience?

Opening Discussion/Warm Up: (10 minutes)
- Assign a word to each corner of the room: compassion, usefulness, friendliness, humane, and have each participant go to the corner that best defines "kindness" for them.
- Why?

I. Kindness is Useful (15 minutes)
a. Is kindness more about "being" or "doing"? What does the Bible say? (James 2:15–17)

b. The Scripture says that "Faith without works is dead." Is it equally true that 'kindness without works is dead?'

c. Are the friendly of the world who don't share kind deeds hypocritical, shallow, or duplicitous?

d. Do you agree with Zig Ziegler's statement, "If you spend your life helping others with what they need, you will always have what you need."

II. What Does Kindness Look Like To God? (25 min.)

a. Read Luke 6:35 out loud. Describe the boundaries of kindness from Jesus' perspective.

b. How does the Good Samaritan (Luke 10:30–37) fulfill Jesus' description of kindness in Luke 6:35?

c. Can you fulfill this standard yourself? Are you supposed to?

d. According to Matthew 5:45 does God observe His own standards when it comes to kindness?

e. If so, does God's kindness equate itself with fairness, justice, or common sense?

III. The Story of Ida Scudder: (20 minutes)

a. Have someone quickly summarize the story of Ida Scudder.

b. Draw a picture of the country you believe needs the most help from missionaries. Explain why.

c. Is the mission field a possibility for you?

d. What would God have to do to convince you of a calling to missionary work?

e. In the mission field what would you

assume to be more effective in winning hearts and minds to Christ
    i.   A precise theology
    ii.   A winsome personality
    iii.   Lots of supplies and programs
    iv.   A genuine kindness/usefulness

IV. Wrap Up (5 minutes)

    a.   Share prayer requests within the group
    b.   Confirm the time and location of the next group study
    c.   Close by reading out loud the following prayer:

Dear God,

You are kinder than I am, and kinder than I will ever fully fathom. Indeed, I cannot possibly comprehend your kindness; too often it looks unjust to me. You send your sunshine upon the just and the unjust and your rain upon those who deserve it and those who don't. Natural disasters strike both good and bad alike. But in it all, Lord, I believe Your nature is always to be kind. Help me welcome Your Spirit, Lord, so that even if I can't understand it I can nonetheless still receive its blessing. In Your Name I pray. Amen

CHAPTER SIX:
GOODNESS

Better Than I Ever Imagined!

I once considered myself to be a good tennis player. I played all the best local players, and won more than my share of matches. I had a big serve and at 6'2" covered the net effectively ... good enough to be cocky. It just so happened, however, that a woman ranked among the world's top 100 on the woman's professional tour practiced at the same tennis facility at which I played. Her name was Jennie Goodling, and she also happened to be our U.S. congressman's daughter. She was young, small, and didn't hit the ball hard at all. Naturally I was curious how I would do against her. One day I got my chance.

Jennie was just finishing her daily practice, and I was scheduled to get on the court next, but my partner was late, so I asked Jenny if she would be willing to play till he came. She agreed and we hit back and forth till I was warmed up. With no sign of my partner, I asked if I could serve a game. She smiled and said "sure." The Bible talks about "a lamb being led to slaughter ... " Well let's just say I presumed she would be the lamb. I launched my nastiest slice ruthlessly into her backhand and rushed the net with vengeance. But Jenny deftly stroked the ball right past me down the line. "Lucky shot" I thought to myself. Again I fired a monster American twist and rushed the net. Once more, she patted it past me with ease. For the next ten minutes I hammered, spun, cut, and sliced every shot I had in my arsenal, and I don't think I won a point. I quickly discovered that what I considered to be good had no relation whatsoever to what the women's professional tennis tour considered good. They were worlds apart.

In the world of religion, folks tend to concern themselves with being good people. Good Jews want to follow the Law of Moses. Good Muslims want to submit themselves to Allah. Good Buddhists want to relieve suffering. And good Christians want to be transformed into the likeness of Christ. Most of the world's religious people would like to consider themselves good, but this is where many get into trouble, because what we consider good and what God considers good are worlds apart!

I. Jesus Gets Into Trouble!

Jesus regularly got Himself into trouble by raising

the bar on goodness, and in so doing He convicted those who thought of themselves as good people. The Jews of Jesus' day were concerned with fulfilling the Laws of Moses. Everything they did was prescribed by one of the 614 laws of the Torah ... what they ate, how they treated others, the way they raised their families. Being a good person was a simple matter of following Moses' Law. But then Jesus came along and turned everything upside down. Let me give you an example of how He did this:

Jesus once taught in a synagogue on the Sabbath. The Rabbis and leaders present found nothing wrong in what He said. Indeed, they were impressed like everyone else. But then Jesus did something that raised the bar on everyone's notion of what was good. It so happened that a man with a deformed right hand was in the synagogue. Seeing him, Jesus asked the Rabbis and leaders around Him,

> "... is it lawful on the Sabbath to do GOOD ... ?"
>
> *Luke 6:9*

Everyone present knew that the fourth of the Ten Commandments specified that no work was to be done on the Sabbath.

> "Remember the Sabbath day, to keep it holy. Six days you shall labor and do all your work; but the seventh day is a Sabbath ... in it *you shall not do any work ...*"
>
> *Exodus 20:8–9*

For the Rabbis and leaders this law was simple ... a good person did absolutely no work on the Sabbath, regardless of whether it was good or bad. But Jesus moved past their interpretation, and directed the man to hold out his deformed hand, whereupon He healed him ... restoring the hand to perfect health. One would assume that everyone present would be thrilled. But Jesus had just violated a basic principle of the Mosaic Law, so some were scandalized. Jesus had done the right thing at the wrong time. This is how the Bible describes their reaction:

> " ... They were filled with fury and discussed with one another what they might do to Jesus."
>
> *Luke* 6:11

The Rabbis and leaders thought they were good people, but then Jesus raised the bar on God's goodness and they all got defensive.

This story exemplifies why some people don't like organized religion. It can raise the bar on what is understood to be good. Here's what I mean. You can consider yourself a good person, but that doesn't mean organized religion is going to agree. You can tell little white lies, steal the government blind on your taxes, and still consider yourself a good person, but that doesn't mean organized religion must agree. No one likes to fall from grace. No one likes having their faults and failures pointed out, which is why some stay as far away from organized religion as possible. If you have a husband or wife who doesn't want to come to worship, or if you have a teenager who doesn't want to come to youth group, it may be because they are holding on to a view of themselves as a good person, and they don't want religion messing around with their self-esteem. Organized religion does have a way of doing that ... of calling into question just how good you really are.

There are, after all, two basic ways of assessing our goodness. First, we can measure it by using popular opinion, and second we can use a more objective standard–God's standard being the most obvious. Popular opinion generally says that a good person is someone who does more good things than bad. But the bar on God's goodness is set much, much higher. Jesus described God's standard for goodness when He said:

> " ... If you do good to those who do good to you, what credit is that to you? Even sinners do the same ... But love your enemies, and do good, and lend expecting nothing in return."
>
> *Luke* 6: 33, 35

God's standard for goodness is infinitely higher than that of popular opinion.

II. No One is Good!

Jesus was once approached by a rich young man who hailed Jesus using the title "good teacher." "Good teacher," the young man asked, "what must I do to inherit eternal life?" It's an obvious question. Just how good do we have to be to get into heaven? But Jesus' response set a surprising standard for what He considered good. He said,

> "Why do you call me good? No one is good but God alone."
>
> *Mark* 10:17–18

Wow! According to Jesus no one is good but God! Like I said, Jesus' standard is much higher than what is commonly thought. It goes way beyond what is lawful, or popularly moral. Indeed, Jesus' standard for whom and what is good isn't even human!

Let me sharpen what the Bible says about goodness. The Scripture clearly states that God does not consider any of us to be good. Let me say this again because it is one of the Bible's most basic spiritual principles. God does not consider anyone good. Not Billy Graham, not the Pope, not the Dali Lama, not anyone. Here is chapter and verse:

> "No one is good but God alone."
>
> *Mark* 10:18

St. Paul amplifies this point when he observes that even when we want to do good, we can't always do it:

> "I can will what is right, but I cannot do it. For I do not do the good I want, but the evil I do not want is what I do."
>
> *Romans* 7:18–19

We've all experienced this to be true. There isn't a person here who hasn't foiled their own good intentions. Good heavens, we don't even live up to our own standards let alone God's. For example, every parent wants to pour only love into their children, but that doesn't mean they always succeed. There isn't a parent alive who hasn't made mistakes with their kids even with the best of intentions. Just because we think of ourselves as good, doesn't mean we always are.

Let me share another example.

I first got married when I was 42-years old, and up to that point I generally considered myself a good person. But once married I was forced to see myself in an entirely new light. Marriage revealed character flaws I never saw in myself, or at least would never admit to myself. It had been easy for me when living alone to hold onto certain illusions about myself as a good person, but my marriage shattered them all. My marriage demanded patience, selflessness, empathy, thoughtfulness, and a host of other virtues I quickly discovered were wanting in me. Please don't get me wrong. I am grateful for my marriage, and I'm confident I am a better man for having married Stephanie. But after eight years of matrimony my cockiness is down and my humility is up, a natural development of eating a steady diet of humble pie. Marriage raised the bar on what I understood goodness to be.

As old Martin Luther once wrote, marriage is the best Christian education available. I suppose

God designed it that way—marriage as the anti-dote to self-centeredness. What I understood to be good when I was single and what I understood to be good after I had been married were worlds apart.

The interpretive key here is to ask "compared to what"?

When God's word says, "You are not a good person," the obvious question is, "Compared to what?"

If you were to say to your spouse, "You are a slob" the obvious answer would be "Compared to what?" Compared to my children I'm quite neat, but compared to a barracks in the U.S. Marine Corps I'm a slob.

Well, God's standard of comparison is always the same ... His standard for what is good is always Himself. He compares you and me to Himself and concludes that no one is "good." God's word has told us this in plain language:

> "... all have sinned and fallen short of the glory of God."
>
> *Romans 3:23*

Most presume themselves to be good. But the sad facts are that none of us rise above selfish self-interest. We are all motivated to one degree or another by "what's in it for me," and this flaw always leaves us short of God's selfless standard for goodness.

When asked, "Are you going to heaven?" Most

people would answer "yes." And when ask "why" they would probably reply, "Because I'm a good person." But the problem is that God doesn't use the standard of popular opinion to define who is good. He isn't impressed with the one who has done more good things than bad. He's impressed with the person who loves their enemy, who turns the other cheek, and who carries a cross for the sake of those who do evil, and every one of us falls short of such a standard.

III. God Can Do It When You Can't!

Many of us have concluded that we just can't live up to God's standard of goodness. The bar is set too high. Like St. Paul said,

> "Even though the desire to do good is in me, I am not able to do it."
>
> *Romans* 7:18, gn

Hard experience has taught us that what we consider good doesn't always measure up. Again, I presumed I was a good tennis player, but little Jennie Goodling showed me what good tennis really was. I thought I was a good man, but my marriage showed me how much better I needed to be. I used to think of myself as a good Christian until I realized just how high Jesus set the bar. This realization would be discouraging but for one thing. Included in God's goodness is a generosity and grace that we can't comprehend! Even when we can't do what is best, God can and will help us.

God just loves to plant His goodness into an open and willing heart, turning the average man into the uncommon saint.

Let me share a simple story that helps to illustrate my point. Stephanie and I were walking down a street in Paris after a lovely evening of the ballet and dinner. While walking we came upon a young man who was so drunk he was passed out on the sidewalk. It was freezing outside, but people were passing him without even a look down at him. I confess that I passed by too. After all, we were in a strange country (France), it was cold, we were tired, my French was only okay, and frankly I didn't want the hassle. But after I passed the voice of the Lord spoke clearly to me, saying, "Isn't this your neighbor?" It was an obvious reference to the Good Samaritan story.

My response inside myself was to say, "Lord, it's late, cold, and dangerous." To which His voice responded, "It is for him too."

To make a long story short, the Lord got me turned around, and we took care of the young man and got him secured. Now, here is the important part. I didn't want to do it. If it had been up to me I would have passed him by. But the Lord had planted His goodness in me, and He would not let me pass him by. The goodness of God interceded for the young man, and also for me. You see not only did God want to care for the drunken young man, but He also wanted to raise me up to higher standard ... He wanted to raise the bar of goodness within me.

Like I've said, I can't always do it. I can't live up to God's standard of goodness. But God can do it in me and through me. Time and time again I have proven to myself that I am not as good as I would like to think of myself as being, but God is exceedingly better than I ever expected. As Jesus Himself said:

> "Truly, truly, I say to you, he who believes in me will also do the works that I do; and greater works than these will he do ... "
>
> *John* 14:12

Scripture tells us that the sixth of God's nine spiritual fruits is the spirit of goodness.

> " ... The fruit of the Spirit is love, joy, peace, patience, kindness, *goodness* ... against such there is no law."
>
> *Galatians* 5:22–23

Notice how St. Paul ends this verse by saying "against such there is no law." There is no law or limit to God's goodness. The Rabbis and religious leaders of Jesus' day tried to stop Him from breaking Moses' Law by healing a man's deformed hand on the Sabbath, but Jesus did not hesitate. And the Good Samaritan helped the wounded Jew by the side of the road, even though it was against custom for the two of them to have contact. The

Lord pushed me past the limits of my own goodness to serve the needs of a drunken young man
lying on the street. We may not have been able to
do it ... but even if it was out of our league, nevertheless God could and would accomplish it through
us. The goodness of God can prevail against our
stubborn self-centered nature.

This is the message in many of the Bible's
stories.

Moses didn't want to return to Egypt after he
had left it 40 years earlier. But God's goodness
prevailed upon Moses to return and lead his people
to freedom against all odds.

King Saul had hunted David down like a dog, and David
had every reason to kill Saul when he had the chance. But
the seed of God's goodness prevailed and inspired David to
spare Saul's life.

The prophet Jonah had no wish to help the people of Nineveh – they were the sworn enemies of
the Jews. Jonah would have sooner drowned himself than help them. But the seed of God's Spirit
prevailed, and Jonah saved thousand of lives in
Nineveh.

Jesus' disciples had no wish to leave their Homes and
families for anyone. They would have preferred to live out
their lives comfortably and obscurely, growing old with
their families. But God's goodness prevailed, and Jesus'
disciples left the comforts of home to share the joy they
had received in Christ.

I can't do such things myself; my 50 years have
taught me that I'm just not good enough. But

experience has also taught me that even if I'm not as good as I thought, God is better than I ever imagined. When His seed is planted into the heart of the average man, His goodness prevails, and the common man becomes the uncommon saint. We become better than we ever imagined.

Using ordinary men to do the extraordinary is just what God intends to accomplish via His Spirit, and there is no better 20th century example than that of Father Maximilian Kolbe.

V. The Story of St. Maximilian Kolbe: Raising the Bar on Goodness!

Maximilian Kolbe was a faithful Polish Priest who was arrested in February, 1941 by the Nazis and thrown into the concentration camp at Auschwitz. There, in the very worst of conditions, he ministered to Jews and Christians alike. He shared his food. He gave up his bunk. He prayed for his captors. By any human measure he was indeed a good man, and he soon earned the nickname "Saint of Auschwitz."

In July of 1941 there was an escape from the prison, and as was the custom at Auschwitz, ten prisoners were chosen to be executed as punishment. All the prisoners were gathered in the courtyard and the commandant randomly selected ten names from the roll book. These victims were to be taken to a cell where they would receive no food or water until they died. One of the prisoners sobbed for his wife and children after his name

Dr. Win Green

was called. He wept bitterly. But then there was a
stir among the other prisoners. Maximilian Kolbe
was pushing his way out of the ranks of prisoners to the front. The guards raised their rifles, the
guard dogs snarled, the officers screamed for him
to return to his ranks, but amazingly no shot was
fired. Kolbe had neither fear on his face nor hesi-
tancy. Upon reaching the front Kolbe calmly said,
"I want to talk with the commander." He stopped a
few paces from the commandant, removed his hat,
and looked the German officer in the eye.

"Herr Commandant, I wish to make a request,
please."

That he was not shot or torn apart by the dogs
was a miracle.

"Herr Commandant, I wish to die in place of
this prisoner." He pointed to the sobbing man. "I
have no wife and children. Besides, I am old and
not good for anything. He's in better condition."

"Who are you?" The officer demanded.

"A Catholic priest."

There was an awkward silence. Everyone was
frightened, and unsure of what to do or say, except
Maximilian Kolbe.

Finally the commandant said, "Request granted."

Father Kolbe was marched off with the other
nine prisoners where they were locked in a cell to
die together. Maximilian Kolbe ministered to each
of the other nine prisoners to the very end. He
himself was the last to die.

A few years ago Saint Maximilian Kolbe was

canonized by The Vatican, and standing at that canonization ceremony was the very man whose place Father Kolbe took at Auschwitz. I'm sure that man presumed he was a good man before he was imprisoned at Auschwitz. But it was there, amidst the worst of human brutality, that the bar for goodness was raised to an entirely new level for him. He learned without the shadow of a doubt that his idea of goodness and God's idea of goodness were worlds apart. Indeed, God's goodness was better than he ever imagined!

Group Study
Better Than I Ever Imagined! (90 minutes)

Introduction (5 minutes)
Briefly:

- Affirm one good thing you can express about each participant in the group. Tell why it is good.

Opening Discussion/Warm Up: (10 minutes)

- Using a news magazine (*Time, Newsweek,* etc ...) show different pictures of various newsmakers to the participants, and have them declare whether they consider the person shown in the picture to be good, bad, or both.
- If the participant's children or parents were asked whether they were good, bad, or both what would they (the children or parents) say?
- Share with the group why you consider yourself to be a good person.

I. Jesus Gets Into Trouble (15 minutes)
a. Read out loud Luke 6:6–11
b. What did Jesus do to get Himself into trouble?
c. Did He raise the standard on what was "good" behavior?
d. Does religion generally raise the stan-

dard for "good" behavior, and do people sometimes resent that higher standard?

e. Read the following statement of Jesus:

" ... If you do good to those who do good to you, what credit is that to you? Even sinners do the same ... But love your enemies, and do good, and lend expecting nothing in return."

Luke 6:33, 35

f. Does this raise your standard for what is good behavior?

II. No One is Good (20 minutes)

a. Divide the room into two halves. Those who consider people to be basically good get on one side of the room, and those who believe people are basically flawed get on the other side.

b. How good does God consider human beings according to Mark 10:18?

c. What does St. Paul think of human goodness according to Romans 7:18–19?

d. By what standard does God compare us ... by the standard of popular opinion or by a more objective standard?

e. According to Romans 3:23 all human goodness falls short of what?

f. Read Acts 5:1–11 out loud together.

g. According to Acts 5, would the secular world today consider the donation of

Ananias and Sapphira to be a good and generous one?

h. What got Ananias and Sapphira into trouble with God?

i. Did God's action with Ananias and Sapphira raise the bar for the rest of the church community (Acts 5:11)?

j. If you were Ananias' or Sapphira's friend or relative, what would you think of the God of Jesus?

k. Take a vote amongst the participants on the question–Was God good/fair with Ananias and Sapphira?

III. God Can Do it When You Can't
(20 minutes)

a. According to Romans 7:18, even when we have the best of intentions can our actions reflect God's standard of goodness?

b. Read out loud John 14:12

> "Truly, truly, I say to you, he who believes in me will also do the works that I do; and greater works than these will he do ... "

> *John* 14:12

c. Read out loud John 15:5

> "He who abides in me, and I in him, he it is that bears much fruit, for apart from me you can do nothing."

> *John* 15:5*b*

    d. According to the above two verses, what is the key to being good and doing good?

IV. The Story of St. Maximilian Kolbe (10 minutes)

    a. Read out loud the story of Maximilian Kolbe from the text.

    b. What does Father Kolbe's story do to raise your understanding of God's goodness?

Wrap Up (5 minutes)

    a. Share prayer requests within the group.

    b. Confirm the time and location of the next group study.

    c. Close by reading out loud the following prayer.

Dear God,

We tend to think more of our goodness than Your own. Indeed, we frequently question Your goodness after a natural disaster or tragic event, prosecuting your lack of action, and calling into question Your very existence. Lord, help us to put our trust in Your goodness. Help us to view life from Your eternal perspective rather than from the secular perspective of the here and now. Help us to understand that Your goodness is not measured in how happy we are, or in how secure and successful our family is, but in how close we come to Christ. For in Christ we will not only see your glory, we will also touch it. The divine will be made human for us, and we will come to know just how deep and wide Your goodness is. Lord, give us the courage to admit just how far we are from what is truly good, and yet give us the eyes to see just how near your goodness is to each of us. Amen

CHAPTER SEVEN:
FAITHFULNESS

*Small Things
Done With Great Love
Change the World!*

At the 2006 Torino Winter Olympics speed skater Joey Cheek won a gold medal in world record time, but what he did after winning gold was even more impressive. With microphones thrust into his face, and the whole world watching, Joey Cheek used his sudden celebrity to focus attention upon the plight of refugee children in Africa. Rather than bask in his victory, he used his moment of glory to pledge his entire $25,000 bonus to help the children of Africa. *The Seattle Times* reported Cheek as saying, "What I do is honestly a pretty ridiculous thing. I mean, I skate around the ice in tights." Wow, what a refreshing attitude. And what a witness. Using his blessing to bless others! Using the opportunity of a world television platform, Joey Cheek seized the moment to lift a vision. He redirected television's bright lights away from himself and onto a greater cause. At the critical moment he proved himself faithful to what he believed.[15]

Being faithful to what one believes is rare, which is why Joey Cheek's example is striking. Good intentions are common, but it's tough to follow through in the face of temptations, trials, and tedium. Even if most people are concerned with poverty in Haiti, street orphans in Brazil, and refugees in Darfur, Sudan, it's tough to remain faithful to their needs when we feel so overwhelmed with our own. We mean well, but we don't always do well.

So how do you remain faithful? How do you remain faithful in your marriage when the passion is down and the boredom is up? Statistics reveal that two out of three husbands, and one out of two wives are unfaithful during the course of their marriage! What's the answer? Likewise, how do you remain faithful in your business dealings, where the temptation to cut corners and fudge numbers is as easy as saying the words: "Everyone else does it?" Above all, how do you remain faithful to God in a world that scoffs that such practice is naive?

Human nature is more fickle than faithful. If 4,000 years of recorded history has proven anything it is that people aren't particularly reliable.

But this isn't to say that there isn't an answer. History is littered with great and small examples of individuals who beat the odds to remain faithful to their convictions. Take the recent news story of twelve year old Jonathan Farmar of Arkansas.

Jonathan gave up a once in a lifetime opportunity to visit his favorite baseball team—The New York Yankees—and instead donated $1,000 of his hard earned savings to help keep his middle school open. Here's the story: The Arkansas Board of Education had threatened to merge Jonathan's middle school with a surrounding district if a budget shortfall wasn't covered by local citizens. Because he believed in his school so much, Jonathan passed on a dream trip with his dad to see his beloved Yankees in New York and instead donated his savings to help his school! His mother said that it was a hard decision for Jonathan to make, but that he prayed about it and concluded it was the right thing to do. Now that's faithfulness to a cause!

And the story has a great ending. Yankee's owner George Steinbrenner caught wind of Jonathan's story and wrote him a letter saying, "Jonathan, I couldn't be more proud of you. It takes quite a man to give up his personal dream for a higher purpose." Steinbrenner then promised to fly Jonathan to New York, give him a personal tour of Yankee Stadium, and the run of the field during batting practice![16]

Remaining faithful to what one believes is possible, but it's never easy. Indeed, it usually requires much prayer and soul searching.

Faithfulness is the seventh fruit of the Spirit. It is of particular interest for our present day because challenges to personal integrity lie at every turn, and the temptation to "me first" living is at an all time high. Faithfulness is a character trait required by anyone living in the 21st century who wants to live a healthy and balanced life. In the following pages I will detail how God's Spirit can empower you to stand firm in your faith so that you can stay true to your convictions and keep your promises!

I. Living a Double Life:

In August of 2004 three adult brothers living in a small Illinois town were challenged in a way they could have never imagined. Before them on a television screen was the video tape of their beloved father–William Ginglen– former marine, former president of the local junior chamber of commerce, and auxiliary police officer, robbing a bank! Never in a thousand years could they have dreamed such a thing was possible, but their dad's robbery was as undeniable as the video tape before them, so they had to decide whether or not to turn in their father. William Ginglen had always raised the boys to do what was right. The moral compass he had preached to them as boys was a simple one, 'what's right is right, and what's wrong is wrong.' Somehow one of the brothers came across the video tape on a public affairs web site, and had recognized his bank robbing father immediately. He called his two brothers and had them watch the video.

The oldest vomited in the waste basket when he first saw the surveillance photos. Further investigation revealed that their father was living a double life, one as a model citizen, and another as a drug crazed, womanizing, thief. Much to their dismay the brothers discovered that the faithfulness they believed to be the norm in their family was anything but. Much to their credit, there was never a question of what the three boys would do. After all, their father had raised them to always do the right thing, and they intended to be faithful to that standard, even if it meant turning in their Dad.[17]

Being faithful is neither easy nor natural. Indeed, it is so hard that some like William Ginglen resort to leading a double life. They're rarely as dramatic as his, but they are double lives nonetheless. For example, some worship at both the local church and the out-of-town strip club. Some spend responsibly with their own money, and liberally with the company's credit card. And some reassure their children of their love, but rarely make room for them on their schedule. Double lives are not evidence of a lack of faith as much as a divided faith. The priorities of one's heart conflict with the priorities of one's self-interest, which in turn conflict with the priorities of one's ideals.

To keep sane, some resort to compartmentalizing, building walls between the different facets of our lives: family, work, worship, friendship, and community. Such walls can easily lead to double lives, in which what we do at home isn't connected with what we do at work, which isn't connected with what we do socially, which isn't connected with our worship. Being faithful in the post-modern world is hard because American culture is so utterly fragmented and disconnected which makes it all but impossible to remain firm and steadfast.

Like I said, faithfulness is not the norm but the exception. "Semper Fi" ('always faithful') may be the motto for the United States Marine Corps, but even the Marines have alumni like William Ginglen who lose their way and prove faithless. The natural response to this challenge is to ask God for more faith. After all, if we struggle with faithlessness wouldn't the obvious answer be more faith? Astonishingly enough this isn't the solution Jesus pointed to.

II. A Little Less Talk, And A Lot More Action!

In the middle of His ministry Jesus' disciples approached Him and made what seemed a reasonable request. They petitioned,

> "Lord, increase our faith."

> *Luke* 17:5

They made their request after Jesus had shared with them a particularly difficult teaching, one they didn't think they could do with the amount of faith that they had. But Jesus' response was not what they expected. His answer was:

"If you had faith as a grain of mustard seed, you could say to this sycamore tree, 'Be rooted up, and be planted in the sea,' and it would obey you."

Luke 17:6

The mustard seed was the smallest of all seeds, and Jesus used it in his parable to say, 'The size of your faith is not what is important. It's how you act on your faith that counts.' His spiritual principle is simple—small faith accomplishes big things. You can have all the faith in the world, but if you don't put it to work, it will accomplish nothing. Conversely, you can be brand new to the faith and feel like you know nothing about it, but if you are willing to act on it, great things can be accomplished! Small faith accomplishes big things!

It's common to assume the soul to be an empty tank into which God pours His faith. When you feel your faith tank is low you pray and attend worship so God can refill your faith tank. But this isn't the understanding Jesus shares with his disciples. Instead He tells them faith is the smallest of God's gifts. Those who receive faith must decide whether or not to attempt big things with it. In other words Jesus distinguishes faith from faithfulness. Faith is what God gives, and faithfulness is how you respond. God gives you the seed of faith, and you respond in one of three ways:

1. You ignore it.
2. You accept it, but do nothing.
3. You accept it, *and* act on it.

Faith is what God gives, and faithfulness is what you do with it. Faith is up to God. Faithfulness is up to you! Unfortunately, this important distinction confounds many believers, for instead of acting on the small bit of faith they have, they waste their time seeking more faith, or they use the excuse that they don't have enough faith to act.

Take for example the woman who wants to start a new business, and who must decide whether to risk leaving the security of her steady job. She can pray all she wants to, but if God gives her the green light and she won't act on it, He's not going to pour more faith into her, for she won't act on what has already been given!

Faith is God's gift, and you don't need a lot of it, you only need the courage to act on what you have. When the Bible says, "The fruit of the spirit is ... faithfulness" it is the courage to act on the faith God gives you. Let me offer another example.

Most Christians hate the word 'evangelism.' They hate it because they don't want to embarrasse themselves. Even when they believe evangelism is essential, still they never get around to actually doing it. Simply put, they have faith, but they aren't faithful witnesses. This being true, it only stands to reason that God wouldn't give such people more faith if they won't act on the faith they have.

Shortly after Jesus' disciples made their request

for more faith Jesus told a story to communicate this distinction between faith and faithfulness.

"A nobleman was called away to a distant empire to be crowned king and then return. Before he left, he called together ten of his servants and divided among them ten pounds of silver, saying 'Invest this for me while I am gone.' But his people hated him and sent a delegation after him to say, 'We do not want him to be our king.'

After he was crowned king, he returned and called in the servants to whom he had given the money. He wanted to find out what their profits were. The first servant reported, 'Master, I invested your money and made ten times the original amount.'

'Well done!' The king exclaimed. 'You are a good servant. You have been faithful with the little I entrusted to you, so you will be governor of ten cities as your reward.'

The next servant reported, 'Master, I invested your money and made five times the original amount.'

'Well done!' The king said. 'You will be governor over five cities.'

But the third servant brought back only the original amount of money and said, 'Master, I hid your money and kept it safe. I was afraid because you are a hard man to deal with, taking what isn't yours and harvesting crops you didn't plant.'

'You wicked servant!' The king roared. 'Your own words condemn you. If you knew that I'm a hard man who takes what isn't mine and harvests crops I didn't plant, why didn't you deposit my money in the bank? At least I could have gotten some interest on it.'

Then, turning to the others standing nearby, the king ordered, 'Take the money from this servant, and give it to the one who has ten pounds.'

'But master," they said, 'he already has ten pounds."

"Yes," the king replied, 'and to those who use well what they are given, even more will be given. But from those who do nothing, even what little they have will be taken away."

Luke 19:11–26, NLT

Jesus' story is a simple allegory. The King is God. The servants are God's people. The silver is the faith God gives. And the response of the different servants represents their faithfulness. Some servants invested what was entrusted to them are blessed with more. But the servant who hid his silver (faith) in a safe place lost what he had. Jesus' story reveals a bias toward action. As the Apostle James wrote: "Faith without works is dead" (James 2:17, paraphrase). Said another way, 'faith without follow through is faithlessness.'

Make no mistake about it, God will test you. He wants to know if you will be loyal and dependable, for if God can't rely on you to act on the little things, He won't entrust you with something big. God is eager to work wonders through you, but first he must know that He can count on you. God tested the faithfulness of Moses with his father-in-law's sheep before He entrusted Moses with the mission of leading the people of Israel out of Egypt. God tested David's faithfulness first as a shepherd, then as a servant to the king, then as a soldier, and finally as a prince before He entrusted David with the Kingship of Israel. And God tested Paul's faithfulness with trial after trial: shipwrecks, whippings, hunger, exposure, betrayal, and imprisonment before God entrusted Paul with the building of new churches. God will test your faithfulness to confirm whether or not His heart beats within your heart.

III. God Is Faithful!

While studying the Bible's use of the word "faith" I was shocked to discover that the King James Bible uses the word "faith" only twice in the Old Testament! Certainly faith is important to the Old Testament message. But having said this, faith is clearly more central to the New Testament, where it is used 308 times.

Faithfulness, however, is more central to the Old Testament, but it is not the faithfulness of men and women. Indeed, The Old Testament recounts the history of how consistently men and women prove less than dependable. Instead, over and over again the Bible's Old Testament confirms God's faithfulness. In fact an over-arching message of the Old Testament is that God is faithful, even when men and women aren't. He can be trusted with confidence. As the Scripture says:

> "The Lord is good, and His love endures forever;
> His faithfulness continues through all generations."

> *Psalm* 100:5

A rainbow reminds us that God is faithful, and that He keeps His promises. Faithfulness always begins with God, for He is the source of all that is firm and dependable, which is just what the hymn writer Thomas Chisholm intended to communicate when he wrote:

> Great is Thy faithfulness!
> Great is Thy faithfulness!
> Morning by morning new mercies I see.
> All I have needed Thy had hath provided;
> Great is Thy faithfulness Lord unto me.

The Old Testament tells us that when the great general Joshua was 110 years old and soon to die, he gathered the leaders of Israel for a final message. He used the occasion to remind them of God's faithfulness. Joshua had seen it all: Moses confronting Pharaoh, God's 10 plagues upon Egypt, the parting of the Red Sea, bread from heaven, water from the rock, fire on the mountain, forty years of provision in the desert, the walls of Jericho tumbling down, and the conquest of the Promised Land. Having seen it all, he wanted to remind Israel of what was most important, so he said:

> "... every promise of the Lord your God has come true. Not a single one has failed."
>
> *Joshua* 23:14

Of all that Joshua could have said as his final message, what was most important was to remind his people of God's firm and secure faithfulness, for upon that Rock they could build their lives, their new country, and their everlasting hope.

God is faithful, and He wants you to enjoy His faithfulness for yourself which is why it is included as the seventh of His nine spiritual fruit. You may not have proven yourself faithful, but God has, and He is eager to share His faithfulness so that you can become a reliable spouse, parent, friend, neighbor, and citizen.

IV. Where Do You Start?

So how do we develop the kind of faithfulness that stands firm in the face of temptation, trial and tedium? When half our marriages don't fulfill the commitment "till death do us part," when we require lawyers for just about everything because we can't be trusted, and when Catholic priests can't remain faithful to the very children they're charged to protect, we obviously have a problem! How do we lift the imperative of faithfulness off the pages of Scripture and make it real in our daily lives?

Mother Teresa once said something both wise

and practical about faithfulness. She said, "Be faithful in the small things, because it is in them that your strength lies." What she said was really just a paraphrase of what Jesus had already taught,

> "Whoever is faithful in small matters will be faithful in large ones."
>
> *Luke* 16:10, GN

The spiritual principle here is obvious: *Do the small things!* It's the small things that build big faith! Just as an Olympic weight lifter builds strength one pound at a time, so too is the strength of one's faithfulness established one small increment at a time. God didn't entrust Moses with his mission to free the Israelites right away. First he proved himself dependable as a shepherd, able to feed and water his sheep reliably. St. Peter wasn't given the keys to the Kingdom right away. First he proved himself able to serve his fellow disciples reliably. It's the small things that lead to the big things. Those who aren't faithful with their tithe to God won't be entrusted with anything great in God's service.

Conversely, those who persist with faithful habits toward God: prayer, devotions, worship, service, and fasting, are likely to be recruited by God for a larger role in His Kingdom. It's the small things that grow big faith. Through the years I've noticed that people are eager to sign up for big, dramatic, one-time enterprises for God-a short term foreign mission, preaching Sunday morning sermon, leading the youth retreat. However, they are less enthused to commit to the daily routine and grind of simple service. Even so, it is the small things that build the kind of faithfulness that God uses to do His greatest work.

Make a commitment to do the little things faithfully. Talk with God regularly in prayer. How else are you going to know what He wants you to do, and who He wants you to be? Take the time to read God's word! There are literally thousands of promises there for you to claim, but you must first know what they are! Put worship first on your weekly calendar. Even if the preacher is boring, and the choir consistently off key, God's blessing is not dependent on either of those two factors. Entrust your tithe to God. Don't hold back. If you are having money troubles it is probably not because you are giving too much to God. God can do more with 90% than you can with 100%. Finally, clear your body's system with a regular fast, and be empty before God. God can't fill what is already full!

It is the small things that build a great faith! As Mother Teresa once observed:

> "How does a lamp burn? Through the continuous input of *small* drops of oil ... What are these drops of oil in our lamps? They are the *small* things of daily life: faithfulness, punctuality, small words of kindness, a thought for others ... "

Faithfulness is much like the mustard seed that Jesus spoke of. It usually involves the smallest of all tasks, but their cumulative effect is irresistible.

No 20th century individual personified the faithfulness in small things more than Mother Teresa. She started her ministry by committing herself to the most insignificant people in the world, and her faithfulness to them quite literally changed the world. Here's her story.

V. The Faithfulness of Agnes Gonxha Bojaxhiu (1910–1997)

Agnes Gonxha Bojaxhiu was the youngest of three children born in Macedonia in 1910. Her Albanian father was a building contractor who was murdered by poison for his political activity when Agnes was only seven, so to survive her mother opened an embroidery and cloth business. Agnes was a small and shy girl who sensed early Christ's love for her. She spent her adolescence involved in activities of her local parish, and guided by a Jesuit priest she became interested in missionaries. At 18 she answered God's call to serve as a missionary nun, and joined an Irish order: the Sisters of Our Lady of Loreto. She trained briefly in Dublin after which she was assigned to India to teach history, geography, and catechism at St. Mary's Bengali High School—a school for girls from wealthy families. She taught there happily from 1930–1944, after which she served briefly as the school's principal. But in 1946 she contracted tuberculosis. Unable to continue at St. Mary's, she traveled to Darjeeling, India for rest and recuperation. But while on her train ride to Darjeeling she sensed her second calling by God, or as she would later describe it "a call within a call ... to leave her convent and work with the poor, living among them." In 1948, the Vatican granted Agnes permission to leave the Sisters of Loretto and pursue her calling to serve the poorest of the poor on the streets of Calcutta. What follows is her own description of how she first got involved with the dying on the streets of Calcutta.

"The woman was half eaten up by rats and ants. I took her to the hospital, but they could do nothing for her. They only took her because I refused to go home unless something was done for her. After they cared for her, I went straight to the town hall and asked for a place where I could take these people, because that day I found more people dying in the street. The employee of health services brought me to the temple of Kali and showed me the 'dormashalah' where the pilgrims used to rest after they worshipped the goddess Kali. The building was empty and he asked me if I wanted it. I was very glad with the offer for many reasons, but especially because it was the center of prayer for Hindus. Within 24 hours we brought our sick and suffering and started the Home for Dying Destitutes."

Mother Teresa went on to become a living saint, recognized the world over for her service to the poor. Her faithfulness to God's call was the kind that wouldn't quit. She didn't fret over the amount of faith she had, she simply had the courage to act on God's leading. Even in the harshest circumstances on earth, this little woman of 4'11" and 90 pounds proved herself reliable over and over again in God's service. Her faithfulness began with the small things ... saying yes to God's call, teaching school children, and staying true to her devotion. It was only later, after she was tested and proved reliable, that God used her to speak to the world. Again and again Mother Teresa always returned to the importance of doing the small things in a life of faithfulness. As she wrote:

> "We cannot do great things. We can only do small things with great love."

Faithfulness is measured in the small things on which we follow through. It's been said that the devil is in the details, but so too are the angels. When we are careful to follow through on the small things, we just might pause and listen closely for the applause of heaven. It resounds for those who prove themselves faithful! Amen.

Group Study:
Small Things Done with Great Love
Change The World! (90 minutes)

Introduction (5 minutes)
Briefly:

- Share a story of how a friend or family member has been faithful to you.

Opening Discussion/Warm Up:
(10 minutes)

- Using a mews Magazine (*Time, Newsweek ...*) hold up pictures of famous individuals and collectively vote on whether or not they give the impression of being "faithful" public servants. Express why or why not.
- What is hard about remaining faithful?
- What are the day to day obstacles?
- What has helped you stay faithful?

I. Living A Double Life (20 minutes)

   a. Is faithfulness in marriage, work, financial affairs, and in spiritual commitments the norm or the exception?

   b. How tempting is it to live a double life–living one way with your family and church friends, and another with your pals?

   c. Do you feel as if you lack faith, or that your faith is divided between various loyalties, interests, and loves?

II. **A Little Less Talk and A Lot More Action (20 min.)**
   a. Is it normal/natural to ask God for more faith (Luke 17:5)?
   b. What was Jesus' response when His followers asked for more faith?

   > "If you had faith as a grain of mustard seed, you could say to this sycamore tree, 'Be rooted up, and be planted in the sea,' and it would obey you." (Luke 17:6)

   Luke 17:6

   c. What is Jesus's solution?
      i. Petition God for more faith.
      ii. Act on the faith you've been given.

III. **God Is Faithful! (20 minutes)**
   a. A basic theme of the Old Testament is God's faithfulness. Sing together the refrain for Great Is Thy Faithfulness

   > Great is Thy faithfulness!
   > Great is Thy faithfulness!
   > Morning by morning new mercies I see.
   > All I have needed Thy hand hath provided;
   > Great is Thy faithfulness Lord unto me.

b. When Joshua was 110 years old and on his death bed he shared a final wisdom with his people. Read it out loud together.

" ... every promise of the Lord your God has come true. Not a single one has failed."

Joshua 23:14

c. When are you tempted to doubt God's faithfulness?

d. What inspires you to trust and act on God's faithfulness?

IV. Where Do You Start? (20 minutes)

a. Mother Teresa once said, "Be faithful in the small things, because it is in them that your strength lies." What are the small things, and why does faithfulness to them generate strength?

b. Read out loud together Luke 16:10 - "Whoever is faithful in very little is faithful also in much." What is the spiritual principle Jesus emphasizes with this verse?

V. The Faithfulness of Agnes Gonxha Bojazhiu (20 minutes)

a. Read out loud the story of Mother Teresa from the text.

b. Did Mother Teresa start with big dreams and ambitions, or did she start with a simple desire to remain faithful to her calling?

    c. Share what you believe your calling is and the challenges you face to stay faithful to it.

Wrap Up (5 minutes)

    a. Share prayer requests within the group

    b. Confirm the time and location of the next group study.

    c. Close by reading out loud the following prayer.

Dear God,

We trust You to be the rock upon which each of us can build our lives. You are solid and steadfast. You are wholly reliable, honest, and true to Your word. It makes no difference, Lord, how faithful we may or may not be. Your character does not change as the circumstances change. You are true at all times, and under all conditions. May we abandon any attempt to go it alone and do it ourselves. Instead, Lord, may we act upon the faith You give us, no matter how small or insignificant it may seem. May we prove ourselves faithful in the small things You set before us. We trust that You can accomplish the things we cannot even imagine. So inspire us to step out in faith, and to be faithful to whatever ministry in which You enlist us. We give ourselves to You, Lord, as our Master, Savior, and Friend. Amen

CHAPTER EIGHT: GENTLENESS

Taming the wild!

In March of 2006, in New York City, a wild coyote was caught in Central Park after a frantic two day chase by police. Somehow this coyote swam across the Hudson River from Westchester County, dodged highway traffic, and wandered into the city. The animal wasn't exactly a threat to people, but neither was it tame enough to remain in the park, where it could terrorize little dogs, eat cats, bark at children, howl at the moon, and generally be a nuisance. The coyote simply wasn't gentle enough for anything but the wild. So, when the police finally caught it they returned it to its native forest.

This message is about gentleness–about taming what is wild. When the Bible says "the fruit of the Spirit is gentleness" it is not using the word as Webster defined it. It is not talking about a mother who is tender with her children, or a nurse who is soothing with a patient. No, the original New Testament word St. Paul chose for gentleness is the Greek word *prautes* (prah–oo–tace) which means meek, humble and lowly. It is the spirit of a wild animal that has been tamed. To break a wild horse is to "*gentle*" it. This is exactly what St. Paul refers to when he says that a fruit of the spirit is gentleness. It literally means to have our wild spirits broken and tamed by God–"gentled" into ready obedience.

I. The Taming of John Newton

If ever there was an example of a wild man tamed by God into a spirit of gentleness, John Newton (the writer of the hymn *Amazing Grace*) was it. Born in 1725 the son of a merchant ship commander, Newton first went to sea at the tender age of 11, where he grew up in the vicious cut-throat world of sailors. Newton quickly adapted, and became a rebellious and combative young man who bounced from one ship's service to another in constant trouble with authorities. At one point he was pressed into the British Navy, but he deserted, and hired himself onto a slave ship, where his knowledge of the sea and his licentious character helped him thrive, and he quickly rose in rank to become a slave ship captain. Newton was a young man who broke every rule in heaven and on earth, a wild ass of a man whom not even the cruelties of the British Navy's chains, stocks, and floggings could tame. But on May 10th, 1748 the vessel Newton captained was caught in a violent storm which was breaking up his ship. Desperate while at his ship's wheel Newton cried out to God, "Lord, have mercy upon us!" and miraculously, his ship and crew somehow survived, but it was the death of John Newton's wildness. Brought face to face with his own death, Newton blinked, and thereafter He turned wholly to God. His wild spirit was at last tamed, and from that point he was reliably obedient, and God was able to use him mightily as a great preacher and priest in the Church of England, and the author of one of the world's most beloved hymns.

Taming what's wild is rarely a soft or delicate process, which is one reason why God's gentleness is not always what we expect. When defining gentleness we tend to reference the soft kindness of our mothers. But the Bible's gentleness is different. It's more obedient than soft, more steadfast than kind, and more enduring than delicate. The Bible's gentleness is that which is receptive to divine direction, no matter how hard the prospect. When St. Paul uses the word 'gentle,' he means the quality of having little or no internal resistance to following God's leading, no matter how difficult. It is to be comfortable with God's undisputed Lordship. It is to be utterly submitted to Christ.

Reading this you might hesitate. After all, if the gentleness of the Christian life is all about submission, it might not seem like Good News. After all, what's attractive about being meek? You may not want to be submitted to a Master! Sounds more like slavery than salvation. If this is how you feel you would be wise to keep in mind what the Lord Himself said in behalf of those who yielded themselves to Him:

> "Blessed are the meek (*prautes*), *for they shall inherit the earth.*"
>
> *Matthew* 5:5

The word "meek" used by Jesus in His Sermon on the Mount is exactly the same word St. Paul uses for the word "gentle." In other words, it is those who are gentled by God who will inherit His blessing.

The Bible tells us that King David grew up as a wild shepherd boy who killed bears and lions for sport, but he was willing to be gentled by the Spirit of God, and God raised him up to be the greatest King of Israel.

Amos was a wild goat herder from Tekoa, but he was willing to be gentled by God, and God raised him up to shake the world as one of His great prophets.

Mary Magdalene was so wild she is described in scripture as having been possessed by seven demons! But she was willing to be gentled by God, and God raised her up to announce Jesus' resurrection to the world.

If you are willing to be gentled by God, there is

no telling into what great enterprise God will pour you. When you are willing to be gentled by God, you will possess this incalculably great promise.

> "Blessed are the *prautes* (meek/gentle), for they shall inherit the earth."
>
> *Matthew 5:5*

Of course it may be that you feel too wild to submit yourself to any master, let alone the Lord. If you do, you might keep in mind that the wild don't live well in the company of others. Just like that wily coyote caught in New York City, the wild must live by themselves in the wilderness. They cannot inherit the blessings of the civilized, let alone the blessings of God. John Newton was a wild ass of a man who eventually came in from the cold. So too were Ishmael, Esau, Samson, Pricilla, Philemon and countless other wild men and women tamed by God so that they could receive all the blessings of heaven! You can, too!

II. Practical Application: Selecting a Husband or Wife

So, the obvious question is, 'What does this talk about gentleness have to do with the day to day realities of life? The answer is everything. Let me use the selection of a husband or wife as my illustration for why gentleness is so critical to your daily happiness.

Imagine yourself getting married, enjoying a beautiful wedding in a lovely chapel, and a sumptuous reception with all your closest friends and relatives at the yacht club, and then a honeymoon in a hidden bungalow on the Left Bank of Paris, or in a bridal suite that opens onto a beach in Hawaii, or in a mountain cabin nestled so deep in the woods even radio waves can't reach it. Your every dream is fulfilled, and bliss is your daily companion.

After your nuptial frolic you fly back to establish your home together. You unpack your suitcases, arrange the furniture, open wedding gifts, greet the neighbors, and host your first dinner parties. Everything is perfect, but then somehow a wild coyote finds its way into your new home, and all hell suddenly breaks loose. You chase it around your house, but it eludes you, turning over lamps, smashing dishes, scratching furniture, shredding fabric ... ! It's a mess! Indeed, the more you chase it, the worse it gets. You have no intention of hurting the animal, but it will not respond to any of your pleas. The coyote is simply out of control because it's wild. It's acting according to its nature, and there is nothing you can do or say that is going to change it. As long as it stays in your house, you will have nothing but chaos and catastrophe.

Now, this metaphor of a wild coyote loose in your home may seem a silly one for marriage, but it's accurate. For you see, lots men and women marry an untamed and wild partner. After all, there can be something mysterious and alluring about a wild young man or woman who enjoys living unrestrained and unfettered, without any earthly master or heaven-sent Lord. They seem to live life free and on their own terms. They answer to no one. They are self-made and proud of it. Such people can be an awful lot of fun because they are not inhibited by the civilities of common convention, nor are they reluctant to break the boundaries of etiquette. They enjoy letting it all hang out, and so can be the spice that enlivens the tedium of the day to day. But it's one thing to enjoy an evening of frivolity with such an unbridled character, and quite another to try and build a life together with them. Trying to build a life together with someone who is untamed and wild is like trying to set up housekeeping with a wild coyote in residence. It just doesn't work.

I don't know how many times I've had teary eyed wives or husbands come into my pastor's office over the last 25 years with a story that goes essentially like this:

'Before I married my husband/wife they were fun and exciting, romantic and endearing. But after we got married they just wouldn't settle down. They couldn't seem to control themselves, and now they've spent more than we can possibly pay off, or drunk more then they can handle, or been sexually active outside our marriage. They're just too wild, and I can't control them. They're ruining my life and they're destroying our marriage!'

Again, as a pastor I've been a witness to this too many times, and can testify that the pain is worse than imagined. The very person who was supposed to be the wellspring of infinite joy turned out to be the source of all sorrow. This happens to well meaning, educated, and sophisticated people who get themselves into a marriage with someone who has never been gentled by God. They do not listen to God's voice. They are not under God's direction. They are their own authority and guide.

A part of the story about John Newton I didn't tell you was that he was in love with a lovely Christian woman long before he ever surrendered himself to Christ. And had he been able to marry her before he was gentled by Christ it would have been hell on earth for her. But John Newton's wife was wise. She knew enough to wait for God to take control of John, before ever agreeing to marry him.

The Bible has this simple advice for the unmarried.

"Do not be yoked together with unbelievers."

2 *Corinthians* 6:14

You know what it is for two oxen to be yoked together – they are fitted into the same harness so that they can pull the plow together. Well, the Bible is clear that you are not to be strapped together in marriage with someone who won't take orders from Christ the same way you will! After all, if you get yoked together with an unbeliever and Christ shouts "pull," you've got a problem. Either you're the one who is going to wind up doing all the work, or the master might just turn you both into beef stew because you can't work well together.

Another translation of this same verse is:

"Do not be mismated with unbelievers."

2 Corinthians 6:14 RSV

When I was a young Christian I used to think this verse was an excellent example of the narrow-mindedness of the Bible. 'After all,' I reasoned to myself, 'why should I limit myself to just Christian girls. After all, I live in the modern world. I can be tolerant–think and let think. If my future wife wants to follow a different religion than my own, I'm certainly open minded enough for that.' Again, as a pastor I've had teary eyed wives and husbands come to my office and lament the day they married a non-Christian spouse. They may love them, but the constant strain they are forced to live with because they follow a different master is withering. Different religions say different things–they define love and marriage differently. They offer different prescriptions for raising children. They offer competing foundations for marriage. And too often the holidays become a strain instead of a celebration, and as for which religion the children will practice–the subject is studiously avoided to maintain the family peace. And of course mothers and fathers in law weigh in with their opinions. So rather than one's religion being a source of purpose, meaning, and warmth, it becomes a nagging source of discord and guilt.

A third translation for 2 Corinthians 6:14 is:

"Don't be teamed with those who do not love the Lord."

2 *Corinthians* 6:14 TLB

No matter what anyone tells you, marriage is more teamwork than infatuation and titillation. You can enjoy all the chemistry imaginable in your marriage, but if you don't work together to clean the dishes, wipe the toilet, and pay the bills, that very same chemistry can explode on you. Like any good team, you must follow the same coach. If you're following Christ and your spouse is following someone or something else, you're going to have different priorities, purposes, and passions. Jesus said it simply, "A house divided cannot stand."

You may be saying to yourself, 'my spouse/companion is an unbeliever and is no wild coyote! He/she is wonderful, talented, sensitive, deep, intelligent, and spiritual. ... ' No doubt this is true, but I have a question. Is there a limit to how close you can become together? Is there a limit to what you can share? The romantics might say that the closest we can get is a perfect kiss. The jaded realist might say that the closest we can get is raw sex. The cynic might say that the closest we can get is a shared bank account. But there are many who would say that the closest we can get is spiritual. We can become soul mates. We can share communion in our inner sanctum, the deepest most intimate place of our being ... the place we reserve for our worship. Such a holy place can be shared only with someone who shares our conviction and belief. It is no place for differences of opinion or tolerance. There, you are either one in Christ or you aren't. There is no fudging or fuzzing the differences. And as wonderful as your boyfriend/girlfriend might be, there is a limit to just how much you can share from the deepest depths of your heart if they don't share your personal relationship with Jesus Christ!

The woman John Newton loved was wise enough to wait for Christ to become Lord of John's heart before she said "yes" to his proposal for marriage. Those of you who are in love with someone who has not submitted themselves to Christ would be wise to wait as well ... that is, if you truly want a soul mate!

In his letter to the Ephesians, St. Paul shares practical advice to Christian husbands and wives. It is this:

> "Submit yourselves to one another out of reverence to Christ."
>
> *Ephesians 5:20*

Said another way, 'Husbands and wives, submit yourselves first to Christ, let Him tame and gentle you, and then you will be able to submit yourselves to one another.' Stephanie and I learned by hard personal experience in the first years of our own marriage that it is all but impossible for two proud people to submit to one's spouse. There are just too many thorny issues involved such as control, money, power, family background, ego, and sex for submission to be either natural or easy. To move seamlessly from being in control of your life while single to surrendering authority on your wedding day is unrealistic. BUT when both husband and wife are first surrendered to Christ it makes that surrender possible. Because I know my wife Stephanie is surrendered to Christ it makes it possible for me to submit myself to her ... because I trust the final authority in her life.

When you consider marrying someone the most important question you can ask is 'Who is the final authority in this person's life?' Is it money? Success? Feelings? Parents? Or the Lord? Who or what has the last word in their life? If the Lord of your life is Jesus Christ–if he is your final authority–if He has gentled and tamed you to the degree that you follow His leadership–then to marry anyone who doesn't share that same commitment is to simply set loose a wild coyote inside your life!

To my readers who are single and female, please do yourself a favor, marry a gentleman. By this I don't mean a man who knows which fork to use when while eating at the Four Seasons in New York City, or someone who opens doors for you, or someone who lays down his coat upon a puddle that you might walk across dry shod. That might be nice, but it misses the essential point. The gentleman I refer to is that man who has been gentled·by Christ, who is quick to follow His direction, and who has no internal resistance to His Lordship.

Notice ladies, I speak of this in the past tense—they have already been gentled. They are not projects. They are not men whom you presume will be ravished and tamed by the allures of your love once they are married. It doesn't work that way. It is not the love of a woman that tames a sinful heart, but only the love of Christ upon the Cross!

Men, you are wise to marry a gentle woman, one who listens to the voice of God! The one who will work with God to grow your character. The one who will discern the special gift God has planted in you, and who will be as committed to your spiritual growth and vitality as you are. Marry the one who whispers your name in prayer, and who dreams the dream of what God can do in you and through you. Marry the one driven by God's ambition, and who is equal to the task of His divine calling. Marry God's girl for you.

The good news is that each of you gets to choose. No other choice will affect your day to day happiness as much as your selection of a wife and husband. Of course we have many criteria for this selection: personality and appearance, education and family background, profession and personal interests, chemistry and convictions. But if you choose to ignore their commitment to Christ, you're only choosing to unleash a wild coyote inside the heart of your home.

The Lord wants to lead you into the Promised Land. He doesn't want you to have to live with misfit coyotes too wild for God's Kingdom. His intention is for each of you to enjoy the blessings of His Kingdom, blessings that are promised to those whose hearts are gentled by Him.

Group Study
Taming The Wild! (90 minutes)

Introduction (10 minutes)
Briefly:

- Divide the room into two halves, one side being for the "civilized" and the other side being for the "wild." Have each participant go to the side they prefer.
- Have each participant express why they prefer civilized or wild.

Opening Discussion/Warm Up: (10 minutes)

- When St. Paul uses the word "gentleness" (Galatians 5:23) does he mean kind, mild, and soft, or does he mean meek, tame, and obedient?
- How easy is it to tame a wild animal?
- How easy is it for God to tame a wild man or woman?
- What must God do to tame someone wild? What is the biggest hurdle?

I. The Taming of John Newton (30 minutes)
   a. Read out loud John Newton's story in the text.
   b. Are violent "storms" the only way God gets the attention of wild individuals like John Newton?
   c. How else has God gotten your attention?

    d. Is being gentle/meek a prized character trait in our culture?

    e. Do you always like the idea of being obedient—at God's beck and call?

    f. What is the biblical promise for those who are meek/gentle according to Matthew 5:5?

    g. Name examples of wild men and women in the Bible who were 'gentled/tamed' by God and who were blessed.

    h. Read Mark 5:1–20 out loud as a biblical example of a wild man 'gentled.'

II. The Gentle and Wild In Marriage (35 minutes)

    a. Can "wild" individuals be fun friends?

    b. Can they be entertaining dates?

    c. Are they easy to live with in marriage?

    d. If an individual is "wild" while they are single, does it stand to reason that they will be tame after marriage?

    e. Is the Bible's message in 2nd Corinthians 6:14 intended to be a straight-jacket or a safeguard?

> "Do not be yoked together with unbelievers."
>
> *Corinthians* 6:14

    f. Would you advise your children to marry a fellow believer or to disregard any concern for spiritual convictions?

g. Is there a limit to how close you can be with someone of a different faith?

h. When considering marriage, a question to be answered is, who is the final authority in my love's life? Is this the most important question? Why?

Wrap Up (5 minutes)

a. Share your prayer requests within the group.

b. Confirm the time and location of the next group study.

c. Close by reading out loud the following prayer.

Dear God,

Part of me associates wild with free, but the more mature side of me knows better. Those who are wild are usually alone. Those who are wild are usually thinking of themselves. Those who are wild are slaves to their own needs. Lord, I want to live for more than just myself. I don't want to be caged by my own thoughts and needs. I want to be able to live in the company of men and women in a way that will contribute positively to others. Lord, help me to accept that my life is not all about me. It's about You and what You can do in and through me to bless others with the things of heaven. Lord, I pray that I will allow You to gentle me so that You might be able to use me for Your great purposes! Into Your loving hands, Lord, I entrust my life. Amen.

CHAPTER NINE:
SELF CONTROL

The Body:
A Good Servant but a Miserable Master!

The Miami Herald reported recently that the average man today is one inch taller than in 1960, but also 25 lbs. heavier! In 1960 an average man's weight was 166 lbs.; today it is 191! The increased height is welcome, but the added weight isn't. Here's the problem: one more inch should not result in 25 pounds more weight. The obvious conclusion is not just that we are getting bigger, but that we're getting fatter ... and not just a little. Recent studies indicate one out of three Americans is overweight to the degree that it will affect their health, which in turn will affect their life style, health insurance premiums, and life expectancy.

You may ask, "What does getting fat have to

do with God and spirituality?" The answer is everything.

I. Who Is Your Master?

A basic spiritual question to ask oneself is this: 'Who is your master?' Or said another way, 'Who controls your life?' Is it your body or your beliefs? Is it the Almighty or your appetites? Is it the God of heaven or the god of your belly? Who has primary control of your life–God or your urges?

This is an all too personal issue for some. You may be one who has experienced the hell of eating disorders—where food completely controls the what, where, and when of your life. Or you may know the hell of being addicted to drugs and alcohol ... when your entire life is controlled by your body's craving. Or you may know the addiction to your appearance ... when your life revolves around the way you look. As a consequence your shopping, exercise, diets, finances, and self-esteem all revolve around the way you assume other people judge your attractiveness. You may know all too well the nightmare of what life is like when your body is your master.

Jewish and Christian faith both spring from the same conviction about the body, that it is good servant but a miserable master. Both Judaism and Christianity start with the conviction that our bodies are good. They help us accomplish amazing feats, and offer us the most delicious pleasures. But the appetites of our bodies, when left undisciplined, can be self-destructive. When our bodies are in charge we will eat ourselves into a heart attack, or lust our way into a divorce, drink and drug ourselves into addiction, sleep our way into poverty, or work our way into a nervous break-down. God gave us bodily appetites, and they are good, but when left undisciplined, they take over and prove to be miserable masters.

On several occasions President George W. Bush, (a confessed exercise freak), has mentioned that "inside of him is a fat man fighting to get out." Many of us know the feeling. Personally, I'm one of those people who can sit down in front of the television and easily polish off a bag of Oreos and a quart of whole milk. Each and every one of us faces exactly the same decision ... will we live to eat, or will we eat to live? Will our body be our master, or will we master our body? Again, this decision doesn't involve just our eating habits, but also our sexuality, work habits, appearance, and overall life style. Again, we will either serve our bodies, or they will serve us.

II. Love Is Self-Control:

God's first eight spiritual fruit were described in the previous chapters. We've now come to the last one: self-control.

> " ... the fruit of the Spirit is love, joy, peace, patience, kindness, goodness, faithfulness, gentleness, *self-control* ... "
>
> *Galatians* 5:22–23

It is appropriate for self-control to be last because it is a product of the previous eight, for if you have love and joy in your heart, peace and patience in your soul, kindness, goodness, faithfulness, and gentleness in your behavior, then self-control will likely reign over your body.

The word "self-control" in the original New Testament Greek is *egkrateia* (eng–krat–I–ah), which means self-restraint. The Greek word comes from two words ... *en* which means in, and *kratos* which means strength. Literally it means "in strength," or inner strength. Self-control is all about inner strength.

When faced with an exciting Monday night football game, a great movie, or a favorite old sitcom that tempts you to stay up late into the night, you need inner strength to put the chips away and get yourself to bed so that you can be in top form for your family and work the next day. And when at the shopping mall and face to face with the perfect pair of shoes that you neither need nor can afford, you need inner strength to walk away so that you can open your Visa bill without fear and trembling at the end of the month. St. Paul promises that *enkrateia* inner strength / self-control will grow inside your heart like fruit on a tree when you allow God's Spirit to plant itself inside you.

Keep in mind that the fruit of self-control is more than just self-discipline. Most mature adults know and understand the necessity for self-control, but this doesn't mean it can be done. Just because

you know how important it is to control your temper doesn't mean you can always help yourself to
do it. Hard experience teaches what the Bible has
been saying all along—self-help alone isn't enough.
We need something more. St. Paul wrote two thousand years ago in Romans that even when we know
the right thing to do, that doesn't mean we will
always do it! There are individuals who command
whole armies and/or who govern entire countries,
but who cannot command their own bodily desires.
President Clinton is the obvious example. He led
our country to financial discipline, but he could
not lead his body to moral discipline. Benjamin
Franklin once quipped, "He is a governor that governs his passions, and he is a servant that serves
them." But even if Franklin wrote this wisdom,
still he couldn't live by it. He was a terrible womanizer. Aristotle once wrote: "I count him braver
who overcomes his desires than him who conquers
his enemies; *for the hardest victory is the victory over
the self.*" Here we have a truth upon which both the
secular and religious world agree ... that the hardest victory is the victory over the self. Personal discipline is the hardest of all. Indeed, Christianity
goes so far as to say that self-help alone can't get
it done. We need God's help, and the Good News
here is that God is more than eager to give us the
help we need to discipline ourselves. The solution
is to:

Walk by the Spirit, not by the desires of the flesh.

Galatians 5:16 paraphrase

When we stand in God's presence at worship, when we let His Word flow through our mind in our private devotions, when we let His heart touch ours in service to others, when we sense His love in prayer, then we will discover the miraculous growth of God's Spirit inside of us. And when God's Spirit grows inside so too will its fruit, the culmination of which is self-control. God's Spirit disciplines His followers beyond their ability to discipline themselves. God doesn't just free us from sin's condemnation; God also frees us from its domination. Being a Christian is not just about forgiveness of past sins, it's about receiving the self-control to avoid and master the sins we face today.

So how does one get God's Spirit of self-control? Well, the good news is that you don't get it, it gets you. The Gospel is this: God and His discipline are looking much harder for you than you are looking for God.

My son Jackson is four-years old, which means he is beginning to assert his independence. But I can assure you that his parents' discipline seeks him much harder than he seeks it. He resists our discipline every step of the way, but we will prevail because we know how valuable discipline is for him. Because we love him, we will discipline him ... and our discipline will enrich him the rest of his life.

To get the Spirit of God and its self-control is simply to allow God's Spirit to get you. There is a great mystery here because God's Spirit touches each of us in different ways. For some it's emotional, and for others it's volitional. For some it comes after suffering great loss, but others experience it quite easily and painlessly. What is important is not how God's Spirit enters your heart, but that you welcome His Spirit and cultivate It when It first knocks. When God takes up residence in your heart He will provide the spiritual seed for whatever self-control you lack.

III. The Help God's Spirit Affords

So let's get practical. How does God's Spirit help you put away the late night bag of Oreos, return the credit card to your wallet, and wipe the porn site off your computer screen? Let me share with you four ways that the presence of God's Spirit helps with self-control:

First, God's Spirit gives you a higher purpose for which to live. Olympic athletes are incredibly disciplined because they have a higher purpose. They don't see themselves saying "no" to potato chips; they see themselves saying "yes" to Olympic gold.

When one has a clear sense of purpose, self-control is much easier to exercise. This is the wisdom St. Paul expressed when he wrote:

> "Every athlete exercises self-control (*egkrateia*)
> in all things. They do it to receive a perishable

prize, but we an imperishable."

1 *Corinthians* 9:25

When the Spirit of God is planted in your heart you will encounter a higher purpose, and, like an athlete in training, everything you do, eat, spend, and say will be influenced by that purpose. As a follower of Jesus you have God's work to do, and when you commit yourself to it you will discover surprising self-control.

Second, God's Spirit will give you a higher perspective. It's easy to get lost in life. Not only do we lose sight of where we are, but we also lose sight of whose we are ... children of God. When we are hungry, sexually deprived, or angry it is easy to lose perspective. But God didn't create us to be enslaved by anything ... especially our bodies. We all have a choice. We can say "yes" to our body's short-term pleasures, or we can say "yes" to the pleasures that last. We can live for today, or we can live forever. When you live a secular life, your perspective is the here and now. But when you live God's life your perspective is higher, wider, longer, and deeper.

Let me give you an example of how practical this is. Most people live together before they get married. They do so because they don't want to wait to enjoy sex ... which means their body is in control. The problem is that studies conclusively show that those who live together before marrying have a higher divorce rate than those who don't. This finding defies common sense. After all, wouldn't those who live together first know better whether or not they are compatible? But the deeper answer is that compatibility is not the biggest problem that leads to divorce. People stay together, not because they are compatible, but because they have the discipline of love. If you are undisciplined before your wedding, you will be undisciplined after the wedding. If your body is in control before marriage, your body will be in control after marriage! Most people don't see this because they want to live for the here and now rather than forever. But God's Spirit gives a higher perspective. It helps you to see where you are and whose you are. You are a child of God, not just a piece of meat that must be satisfied.

Third, God's Spirit offers a higher affection.

It is astonishing what happens to a bad boy when he falls in love with a good girl. Suddenly the boy's speech, behavior, dress, and attitude improve because he has a higher affection. His love for a girl lifts him up more than his friends who take him down.

The same thing happens when we fall in love with God. Suddenly we have a higher affection. It doesn't mean that we stop loving late night Oreos, porn, or shopping. It means that we love God's life more. Sin isn't ripped out of the human heart. It is crowded out. True love can fill the human heart to the degree that there is no longer any room for anything else. The discipline of God comes not by crushing our desires, but by allowing the desire for God to crowd out all other desires.

The Bible tells the story of a woman caught in adultery, who was then thrown before Jesus by her accusers. They said to Him, 'Teacher, the Law of Moses commands us to stone such an adulteress, what do you say?' Jesus' answer was simple, 'Let he who is without sin cast the first stone.' One by one the woman's accusers all left, leaving her alone with Jesus. He asked her, 'Is there no one left to accuse you?' She said, "No one, Lord." "Then neither do I." He said. "Go, and do not sin again." The Bible does not say this, but I doubt whether the woman ever did sin again. It's not because she grabbed hold of herself and forced herself to discipline her desire. No. She was able to discipline herself because she fell in love with God. She acquired discipline because her body was no longer in control. It was her love for God that was in control – a higher affection.

So, higher purpose, higher perspective, higher affection, and there is a **fourth,** what I call higher life.

There are times when self-control simply comes and there is no explanation. Its not logical or rational ... it's just mystical. It simply comes out of nowhere. God does what He does. He has His reasons. We don't always have the means to understand. There are moments when God finds us in our moment of need and gives us the presence of mind and self-control to do what needs to be done.

The Bible's Book of Acts tells us that when Jesus' disciples were arrested and forced to stand trial before the authorities, they were able to speak with amazing clarity and possess total self-control. So disciplined were the disciples that even their accusers could not help but be impressed. The Scripture describes the reaction of their captors this way:

> "They couldn't take their eyes off them—Peter and John standing there so confident, so sure of themselves! Their fascination deepened when they realized they were laymen with no training in Scripture or formal education."
>
> *Acts* 4:13, MSG

Sometimes God's self-control just comes. We may not deserve it. We may not even be prepared for it. But God doesn't give His Spirit because we are deserving or prepared. He simply gives it, and it is our choice whether or not to accept it.

Self-control is sorely needed in our 21st century world. Day by day we are getting fatter, more debt ridden, and increasingly more addicted to a wide range of compulsions such as alcohol, porn, and work. Our culture knows the importance of self-control, but the problem is that we just can't do it. We know what is right, but sometimes we're powerless to get it done! But this is not a new phenomenon. Self-control has never been easy or natural for anyone. People have always struggled with discipline, which is why it is always so surprising when someone actually breaks through their human malaise and achieves real temperance. This is just what happened in Dayton, Ohio in the spring of 1935.

IV. The Story of William Wilson & Dr. Robert Smith:

What would you say is the greatest achievement of the 20th Century? You might be tempted to think of victory in the two World Wars, or the development of atomic energy, or the advances of democracy. Personally, I think the greatest achievement occurred in Dayton, Ohio in the spring of 1935, which is when and where Alcoholics Anonymous began ... better known as AA. Think of it, before 1935, if you were an alcoholic you had no hope for self-control whatsoever. If you were an alcoholic you would literally drink away your family, your home, your job, your financial security, your health, and eventually your life. But, with the beginning of AA, millions of lives have been saved. Statistically one out of every ten people is an alcoholic, so we are talking about hope for hundreds of millions of people ... thirty million in the U.S. alone. There is now hope for millions because of what happened at Dayton, Ohio in 1935! ...

The story of how Alcoholics Anonymous began is this. Bill Wilson, a businessman from New York City had all but ruined his life through drinking. He had tried everything to stop, but just couldn't. While on a business trip to Dayton, however, he met a doctor who was also suffering from alcoholism and together, while talking and sharing their experiences, they stumbled upon a spiritual insight that literally saved their lives. Their insight was this ... to admit they were powerless to save themselves. They were not the masters of their bodies; rather their bodies' cravings were their masters. Bill Wilson and Dr. Bob Smith were smart, well-educated men whose lives were being destroyed because they just couldn't stop drinking. Their compulsion to drink was stronger than their willpower, their intellect, their love for their family, and their common sense. Their compulsion to drink was stronger than anything they had to resist it. Their bodies were their undisputed masters.

You might be tempted to say, "What sort of spiritual insight is it to believe in one's powerlessness?" Well, this is the very first message of Jesus' greatest Sermon:

> "Happy are the poor in spirit, for theirs is the Kingdom of God."
>
> *Matthew* 5:3

In other words, Jesus says, happy are the spiritually poor—happy are those who know and accept their spiritual poverty and powerlessness. The Phillips translation of the Bible gets it right:

> "How happy are those who know their need for God, for the Kingdom of Heaven is theirs."
>
> *Matthew* 5:3, *Phillips*

To be spiritually poor is to accept your need for God. It is to recognize that some of your problems are beyond you. It is to admit and accept that you need greater power than your own to possess the self-control God intended you to enjoy. Your problem may be food, credit cards, pornography, or any one of countless compulsions that conspire to ruin your life when your body is in control. Jesus began His greatest sermon with a basic spiritual principle: "Happy are those who accept their need for God."

Of course no one likes to admit defeat, and admitting powerlessness can feel like defeat. Every instinct inside of us rejects the idea of waving the white flag. But it's only when we accept our powerlessness to overcome certain problems that we take the first steps toward real self-control. Little progress can be made in any aspect of our lives: financial, relational, or spiritual as long as we deny our weaknesses, faults, and failures. After all, a chain is only as strong as its weakest link, and inside every one of us are weak links that consistently subvert us. To be too proud to admit our flaws is to be forever betrayed by them. Remember, the Titanic sank because some weren't willing to admit it had any weaknesses.

Again, most of us revolt at the idea of acknowledging weakness and confessing failure. We want to appear to be in control. We want people to think that we have it together. We comfort ourselves with the thought that we can solve our own problems. We live in a self-help culture, and are bombarded all the time with phrases like, "Believe in yourself," "You can do it," "you've got what it takes," "stop listening to those negative tapes." As a consequence we delude ourselves into believing we can handle all our problems. But this just isn't true. The statistics are in, and the evidence shows we aren't handling our problems well at all. Our marriages are disintegrating in divorce court. We are adrift in a sea of credit card debt. The average American is heavier today than in 1966. The world is on fire with war, poverty, and disease. The truth is our problems are getting the best of us, and until we accept our need for that which is greater than ourselves self-control will elude us.

Regrettably, few will confess anything before first experiencing severe pain or trauma. Most have to hit bottom first before they will ever start looking up. Pain is the great spiritual teacher. But some will do all they can to deny pain's obvious lessons, and by doing so they get sicker and sicker, drifting further and further away from God. Others, however, listen to their pain and what it is trying to teach them. Pain either drives people closer to God or further away, and with the first words of His greatest sermon Jesus blesses those who choose to listen to their pain and allow themselves to become poor in spirit:

> "Happy are those who know their need for God, for the Kingdom of Heaven is theirs."
>
> *Matthew 5:3, Phillips*

In other words, happiness is not for those who are far from problems, but for those who are near to God. Happiness is not for those who have no weaknesses, but for those whose strength is God. Happiness is not for those who feel no pain, but for those who can feel God. "Happy are those who know their need for God, for the Kingdom of Heaven is theirs."

Most, if not all, rebel at the prospect of surrendering control. Even so, this is Jesus' prescription for happiness and self-control. By blessing the poor in Spirit Jesus says, 'swallow your pride, and surrender control to Me!'

This is just what Bill Wilson and Dr. Bob Smith did in the spring of 1935. They swallowed their pride and surrendered control to God. They were broken, beaten, and utterly defeated men, who had no self-control whatsoever. But then they discovered that by sharing their weaknesses ... by admitting their poverty of spirit to one another ... by recognizing their need for God ... suddenly God Himself showed up in power and did for them what they could not do for themselves. Suddenly they become men possessed with extraordinary self-control. Millions of recovering alcoholics living lives of sobriety and serenity have since discovered this same spiritual principle to be true for them as well. It has worked for them, and God promises it will also give you to self-control!

Group Study:
The Body,
A Good Servantbut a Miserable Master!
(90 minutes)

Introduction (5 minutes)
- When a restaurant serves more food than is sensible to eat, what do you do?
- Eat it all and risk stuffing yourself
- Ask for a take home bag
- Leave the leftovers on your plate
- Offer your leftovers to your dinner partner
- Other

Opening Discussion/Warm Up: (5 minutes)
Break up into pairs and discuss the five senses: hearing, seeing, tasting, touching, smelling. Which one:
- Gave you the most pleasure when you were 8 years old?
- Got you into the most trouble when you were 21-years old?
- Connects you most effectively with God now?

I. Who Is Your Master? (25 minutes)
    a. Read aloud the following statement:

    "Who controls your life? Is it your body or your beliefs? Is it the Almighty or your appetites? Is it the God of heaven or the god of your belly? Who has primary control of your life–God or your urges?"

Question: If today more Americans are obese, pornography is epidemic, adultery is common, and credit card debt is rampant, who or what controls the lives of many Americans–God or our human appetites?

b. Read Philippians 3:18–19 out loud

"For many…live as enemies of the cross of Christ. Their end is destruction, *their god is the belly*…"

Philippians 3:18–19

When the Scripture refers to the "god of the belly" who or what is it talking about?

c. Read aloud 1st Corinthians 6:19–20 below:

"Do you not know that your body is a temple of the Holy Spirit, who is in you, whom you have received from God? You are not your own, you were bought at a price. Therefore honor God with your body."

What changes must you make to honor God with your body as the temple of the Holy Spirit?

II. Love Is Self-Control: (20 minutes)

a. The word "self-control" in the original New Testament Greek is *egkrateia* (eng–krat–I–ah), which means self-restraint. The Greek word comes from two words... *en* which means in, and *kratos* which means strength. Literally it means "in strength," or inner strength. Self control is all about inner strength. According to the following Scriptures from where does this inner strength come from?

"Walk by the Spirit, not by the desires of the flesh."

Galatians 5:16, *paraphrase*

"But the Lord said to me, "My grace is sufficient for you, for my power is made perfect in weakness."

2 *Corinthians* 12:9

b. According to the scripture below is self-control about:

   i. Developing stronger will power
   ii. Dying to self and allowing Jesus Christ to live in us?

"In the same way, count yourselves dead to sin, but alive to God in Christ Jesus. Therefore do not let sin reign in your mortal body so that you obey its evil desires. Do not offer

the parts of your body to sin, as instruments
of wickedness, but rather offer yourselves to
God, as those who have been brought from
death to life; and offer the parts of your body
to him as instruments of righteousness. For
sin shall not be your master, because you are
not under law, but under grace."

Romans 6:11–14

III. The Story of William Wilson & Dr. Robert Smith: (10 minutes)

a. In what way does the story of William
Wilson and Dr. Robert Smith illustrate
the message of Jesus's first beatitude
from His Sermon on the Mount?

"How happy are those who know their
need for God, for the Kingdom of
Heaven is theirs."

Matthew 5:3, Phillips

IV. Summary Party: (20 minutes)

a. Have each participant draw a symbol for
the spiritual fruit they would like to see
the Holy Spirit grow in them, and how
they plan to "abide in the vine." The
then should "mingle" with their draw-
ing sharing with others what they have
learned about themselves and their spiritual growth. (Drinks and Hors d'oeuvres
can be served).

V. Wrap Up: (5 minutes)

    a. Share prayer requests within the group

    b. Confirm the time and location of the next group study.

    c. Close by reading out loud the following prayer:

Dear God,

We thank you, Lord, for keeping our group together, and for cultivating Your spiritual fruit to grow within us! We pray we are humble enough to accept our need for You, and that we would put aside all the idols our five senses crave to worship, so that complete control might be entrusted to you. Establish Your throne at the very center of our hearts that You might reign over us, setting us free from all the vain things that would deceive and enslave us. Put to death our selfish self-centeredness, Lord, that we might live for a higher purpose than our own immediate pleasure! Lord, You are the source of all that satisfies the human heart, mind, soul, and body, therefore, into Your Lordship do we entrust ourselves. Amen.

CHAPTER TEN:
SPIRITUAL GROWTH

Cultivating A Spiritual Life:

I f I've heard it once as a pastor, I've heard it 153 times ...

"We're not going to raise our children in any particular religion. I'm Catholic and my wife is Jewish, or I'm Christian and my husband is undecided ... so we won't bias our kids with any specific religion. Instead, we'll give them the freedom to choose for themselves."

Like I've said, I've heard this time and again by smart, devoted parents. But this approach raises a question: 'How can children exercise the freedom to choose their religion without the intellectual and spiritual tools to do so?' Inviting kids to define spiritual truth for themselves without first giving them a spiritual foundation to do so is like asking them to read Shakespeare without first teaching them their ABC's.

There is something else I've heard over and over again by well meaning parents: "We're not going to force our children go to our Church's youth group, Sunday school, or confirmation class. We're going to leave it up to them to decide how they want to grow spiritually."

This seems like an enlightened attitude. After all, religion forced down the throats of children and especially teenagers is a turnoff. We risk doing damage by forcing our kids to attend religious programs they want nothing to do with. But it is also true that if we do nothing to train up our children spiritually, then they will be vulnerable to the darker and more sinister forces that lurk in our cultural shadows. In a spiritual free market such as what we enjoy here in the United States there are lots of different religious options and opportunities available to kids, which is a wonderful choice to have, but not all are desirable. So, if we force them to religious programs like Youth Group or Sunday School, we risk turning them off. But if we do nothing, we risk leaving them vulnerable, and without a spiritual foundation.

In an open society like ours it is understandable not to want to bias children spiritually. In an ideal world they might be able to decide their own spiritual path. But are we doing our children a favor by offering them nothing in the way of spiritual training? Nature abhors a vacuum, and our children's hearts and souls will not stay empty for long. If we don't fill our children's spiritual inclinations, you can bet someone else will.

Allow me a simple metaphor.

If I were to clear a plot of land for a garden but plant nothing in it, reasoning that I wasn't going to bias the plot with any particular kind of seed, but rather just let it grow what it wanted. Such an approach would ensure that nothing but weeds would thrive.

A garden must be cultivated if it is to grow something of worth. Using this same logic, a mind must also be schooled if it is to be able to think something of worth, just as a heart must be nurtured if it is to believe something of worth. The Bible testifies to the essential importance of a child's spiritual development:

"Train up a child in the way he should go,
And when he is old he will not depart from it."

Proverbs 22:6

Can you imagine choosing not to educate a child to avoid biasing his or her mind in any way? This is unthinkable, but some choose to do nothing for their child spiritually. This course of action, or inaction, is justified with the rational that children must be tolerant of all religions, *but* again if they aren't given the tools to help them discern their own spiritual convictions or to make sense of their own spiritual experiences, will they grow to be tolerant or simply ignorant?

Unfortunately, many parents today just don't like the spiritual options available to them. They may want to offer their child a spiritual foundation, but they don't like the religion of their parents, they're suspicious of organized religion, they are afraid of cults, they're turned off by the popular religion of TV and radio, they don't know many religious people they trust who might answer some of their questions, and frankly they'd rather sleep in on the weekend rather than drag themselves and their family to a worship service that is too often boring, nonsensical, and irrelevant. Really, the whole religious enterprise seems like more of a headache than its worth. So many just stay at home, throw the blankets over their head, and occasionally preach tolerance.

But a deeper truth may be that "tolerance" too often masks an inability on the part of parents to decide for themselves just what they do and do not believe. Our post-modern world is full of ambivalence toward religion, and with justification. Frankly, the Catholic and Protestant churches of America have done a lousy job as examples of the life of Christ. For this and other reasons families speak little of God at home. God may have planted eternity into our hearts, but that doesn't guarantee that American families are going to talk about it.

But this kind of *laissez-faire* attitude toward spiritual matters is new to history. Most cultures throughout the ages worked hard to cultivate the hearts and minds of its people, especially its children. America is no different. Its history abounds with American men and women who dedicated their lives to sow God's seed into the hearts and minds of their fellow Americans. Jonathan Edwards, Sojourner Truth, Clara Barton, Billy Sunday, Elie Weisel, to name a few. There are many such biographies of great men and woman who cultivated their spiritual life, and in so doing, spread spiritual health and well being to those around them. But perhaps no person so personifies American spiritual cultivation than John Chapman who was born at the birth of America in 1774. You know him as Johnny Appleseed.

I. The Story of Johnny Appleseed:

Johnny Appleseed roamed the Northwest Territory of Ohio, Michigan, Indiana, and Illinois for nearly fifty years planting seeds with a dream–a dream for a land where blossoming apple trees were everywhere and where no one was hungry. His story is no American myth, but the real life of one John Chapman, born September 26th, 1774 in Leominster, Massachusetts. His father, Nathaniel Chapman, was a minuteman who fought the British at Concord. His mother, Elizabeth, died of tuberculosis just three weeks after giving birth to Johnny's younger brother Nathaniel, Jr. His grandparents raised Johnny while his father fought in the Continental Army. He received a good education, and by the time he was 25-years old he learned the trade of a nurseryman in western Pennsylvania and New York.

"Johnny Appleseed" did not just scatter seeds as is popularly believed. He was a practical nurseryman. He knew there was both need and opportunity for supplying seeds and seedlings to those who settled the American frontier at the start of the 1800's.

His business approach was simple. He would buy seeds from cider mills in Western Pennsylvania and transport them into the wilderness first on canoes and then by foot. There he would find the best acreage for planting. He'd clear out the land by hand, cutting brush and pulling weeds. He would then build a brush fence around the area to keep out straying animals, and plant his seeds in ordered rows. Some of his nurseries were small, and some were several acres in size. Once his plantings took root Johnny would sell the seedlings for a few pennies to settlers traveling west. They in turn would plant the seedlings near their homesteads and bring Johnny's vision into fruition of a wilderness blossoming with apple trees.

Johnny did all his work himself, and lived alone for weeks at a time, but never carried a weapon of any kind, for he was a deeply devout Christian. He was a self-appointed missionary for the Church of the New Jerusalem. He shared tracts and Bibles with any settler who would listen to him. On the frontier he was known as friend to settler, Indian, and animal alike. He was often called upon to settle disputes between settlers and Indians, both having confidence in his impartial integrity. He became known to locals as "the apple tree man," which in time became Johnny Appleseed.

It is anyone's guess just how many millions of seeds Johnny planted in the hundreds of nurseries he cultivated south of the Great Lakes. But this much is certain: Johnny Appleseed was a man who cultivated his spiritual garden, and in so doing helped to transform the wilderness of the American Midwest, both spiritually and horticulturally.

John Chapman's life story is an illustration of what it means to cultivate one's spiritual garden. He didn't leave his boyhood home in Massachusetts with the idea of becoming an American legend. He only left with the idea of simply following Christ, trusting the Lord to make his life fruitful, which He did indeed.

II. Cultivate Your Spiritual Garden

My message here is very, very simple. It is to remind you that time and effort are required to cultivate the spiritual life, especially the spiritual life of children. *It doesn't grow by accident!* Like any living thing a soul requires constant care and nurture. There are no short-cuts. Just as it was for Johnny Appleseed, growing spiritual fruit requires starting with good seeds. You have to clear the brush away. And lots of water and sunshine are required. What Johnny Appleseed did in the American wilderness is really no different than what we are called upon to do inside the wilderness of our own hearts. Our hearts are full of brambles and weeds that choke off the things of God that might grow. Lots and lots of clearing must be done in the heart: lies and lusts, pride and prejudice, greed and gossip. These must be cleared for our souls to be healthy.

Unfortunately, too many people assume that a healthy soul is the norm. But a healthy soul is not the norm, it's an achievement! It's the achievement of prayer, worship, spending time with God's word, and serving others. There are no shortcuts! To assume that our children are going to be spiritually healthy because they're acting like everyone else isn't good enough, because study after study tells us that our children are troubled. Many are fat. More are stressed. Drugs and alcohol continue to plague our youth. Suicide is now a primary cause of a teenager's death. Many are not performing well at school. Most teens no longer eat dinner with their families at the dinner table. Kids are in contact with everyone via their computers and cell phones, but they're intimately connected with virtually no one. Deep meaningful relationships are not always part of their day to day lives, hence they are famished for something real and meaningful. Many are hungry for God, but because of our poor example they are turned off by religion.

Now let me ask you, if you were to describe your family's spiritual life as a garden, what would it look like right now? Would it be lush and green, with lots of flowers, new buds, and few weeds? Or is it a chaotic overgrown mess, with vines choking trees and weeds overtaking flowers? There are all sorts of people who don't bother to cultivate their souls, but as the age old wisdom proclaims:

"Ye shall reap what ye sow."

Galatians 6:7

What you plant is what you will harvest. Garbage in, garbage out. Jesus Himself expressed it more elegantly:

"A healthy tree cannot bear bad fruit,
and a poor tree cannot bear good fruit."

Matthew 7:17, gn

Now I am not suggesting that we are solely responsible for what our children become. We're not. Nevertheless, what we pour into the hearts and souls of our children will go a long way to determining how spiritually healthy they will be.

Jesus once told a story of a farmer sowing seed, which has obvious spiritual implications for spiritual growth and health. He said:

"A farmer went out to sow His seed. As he was scattering the seed, some fell along the path, and the birds came and ate it up. Some fell on rocky places where it did not have much soil. It sprang up quickly, because the soil was shallow. But when the sun came up, the plants were scorched, and they withered because they had no root. Other seed fell among thorns, which grew up and choked the plants, so that they did not bear grain. Still other seed fell on good soil. It came up, grew and produced a crop, multiplying thirty, sixty, or even a hundred times."

Mark 4:3–8

Jesus' message is simple. Seeds grow when they are planted in good soil. This is true in nature, and it is just as true in the spiritual life. The Spirit of God grows in our hearts when we break up the hard ground of indifference, remove the rocks of hard heartedness, and weed out our various sins of choice. In other words, time and effort are required to cultivate a healthy soul. And children are in special need of help in this enterprise. Kids don't naturally gravitate to discipline and devotion. They need help here, and the Bible directs adults, especially parents, to help them.

III. What The Bible Does & Doesn't Say About Children:

So just what does the Bible say to parents? According to Scripture just how are parents to cultivate their children's spiritual life? Actually, it doesn't say a whole lot, but what it does say is quite clear and strong. It says we are to:

> *"... tell to the coming generation the glorious*
> *deeds of the Lord and His might."*

Psalm 78:4

We do a lot of talking in our homes about politics, current events, shopping, food, relationships, etc ... One of the basic ongoing conversations parents are to sustain with children is about the Lord and all that He has done, is doing, and will do. Parents are to help their children see the activity of God in the world, and talk it up to our children!

> "And these words which I command thee ... thou shalt teach them diligently unto thy children."

Deuteronomy 6:6

Notice what this verse doesn't say. It doesn't say "thou Sunday School teachers shalt teach them diligently unto thy children." The verse puts the responsibility for teaching children the Bible squarely upon adults, and especially upon the parents. As a pastor I can't tell you how many times parents "drop off" their child at church so that we at the church will "teach them morals." But the Bible doesn't give that responsibly to the Church. Parents are the first and primary teachers for a child's spiritual growth and moral development.

> "Correct thy son ... "

Proverbs 29:17

Parents are not doing their children any favors by being soft on correction and discipline. Children require clear boundaries, and when those boundaries are violated they need consistent correction.

"A soft answer turns away wrath, but harsh words stir up anger."

Proverbs 15:1

Unfortunately, too many parents use their screaming as the primary consequence that their children suffer for doing something wrong. But the Bible counsels just the opposite. It stresses that loud/angry words just tend to stir things up.

"...he who loves him (son) is diligent to discipline him."

Proverbs 15:1

But if parents are to use soft words, they are also to employ clear consequences for misbehavior! The Scripture is not squeamish about our children suffering an appropriate consequence for an inappropriate behavior. But is this the green light for abuse? The following verse would dispel any such notion.

" ... provoke not your children to wrath, but bring them up in the nurture and admonition of the Lord."

Ephesians 6:4

Parents are to correct our children, not abuse them in any way. All correction must come from a motivation of love ... wanting the children to grow and develop into the finest person God created them to be. Far from inspiring hostility, parents are to inspire respect, obedience, and gratitude.

"Children ought not to save for their parents,
but parents for their children."

2 Corinthians 12:14

This seems like an odd notion for the Scripture to stress for parents until you consider our national debt. Collectively, we parents are robbing our children's generation blind, and it is a disgrace! It is the parents who are to pay for the child, not the child who is to foot the bill for the parent!

"Unless the Lord builds the house, those who build it labor in vain."

Psalm 127:1

Parents are not the source of a family's health and well being. In all things the family generally, and each individual in the family must be rooted in their own relationship with God, for "every perfect gift comes from above."

And just what does the Bible *not* say about raising children? It says little about the importance of sports, music, or the importance of getting an education. Instead it emphasizes of the importance of gaining wisdom. It doesn't speak of a child loving or even liking their parents, only of the profound influence of a parent loving their children. It doesn't mention what to feed a child, the schedules they should keep, or the stages of their development, only that parents have a God-given responsibility to discipline them carefully and lovingly. It doesn't say that children are the possession of the parents, but that both child and parents are the possession of God. It doesn't say that children are born with the ability to love. It says just the opposite ... that children are born selfish and self-centered, and that they need to be taught how to love. It doesn't say that children are born with God in their hearts. It says that each child must choose God for themselves, and that we as parents are not to hinder our children in any way from knowing God.

IV. Action Steps:

Everything I've pointed out from scripture boils down to a couple simple action steps. They're not complicated, but neither are they easy to do because they go against the grain of popular culture, and so require devotion. Here they are:

- Eat one meal a day together as a family sitting around the table.
- Pray with your kids.
- Worship together.
- Talk with your children about God at home.
- Read Bible stories together.
- Speak softly when you correct children and follow through with discipline.
- Don't be surprised when your child does something wrong or bad, and praise them when they do something right!

Group Study:
Cultivating a Spiritual Life (90 minutes)

Introduction (5 minutes)
Briefly:

- Share any humorous experiences you've had gardening.
- You could sing together the old spiritual: *In the Garden*

"I come to the garden alone,
While the dew is still on the roses;
And the voice I hear,
Falling on my ear,
The Son of God discloses.
Chorus:
And He walks with me,
And He talks with me,
And He tells me I am His own,
And the joy we share as we tarry there,
None other has ever known."

(C. Austin Miles)

Opening Discussion/Warm Up:
(10 minutes)
Read Psalm 1 aloud and discuss how it reflects the effort and benefits of cultivating one's spiritual life.

I. Change Is Inevitable, Growth Optional
Optional (15 minutes)

a. Do you feel good about your spiritual

growth keeping pace with the changes and innovations that confront you, your family, and your community? What's been your best source for spiritual growth in the last year?

II. Sowing God's Seed: (5 minutes)

   a. Read Jesus' parable of the sower out loud to each other (Mark 4:3–8)

   "A farmer went out to sow his seed. As he was scattering the seed, some fell along the path, and the birds came and ate it up. Some fell on rocky places where it did not have much soil. It sprang up quickly, because the soil was shallow. But when the sun came up, the plants were scorched, and they withered because they had no root. Other seed fell among thorns, which grew up and choked the plants, so that they did not bear grain. Still other seed fell on good soil. It came up. Grew and produced a crop, multiplying thirty, sixty, or even a hundred times."

   Mark 4:3–8

   b. Where do you see yourself in Jesus' parable? Are you the sower, the seed, the birds, the sun, the abundant crop, or one of the different types of soil? Appoint different corners and spots in the room for different identities, and have participants go to the identity with which they relate (sower–to one corner, seeds to another, birds to the kitchen …)

III. Gardens Require Work: (15 minutes)
   a. Read Galatians 5:22–23 aloud:

   "But the fruit of the spirit is love, joy, peace, patience, kindness, goodness, faithfulness, gentleness, self-control; against such there is no law."

   b. Which of these nine fruit are you most eager to grow within you?
   c. Read Galatians 5:19–21 aloud:

   "Now the works of the flesh are plain: fornication, impurity, licentiousness, idolatry, sorcery, enmity, strife, jealousy, anger, selfishness, dissensions, party spirit, envy, drunkenness, carousing, and the like. I warn you, as I warned you before, that those who do such things shall not inherit the Kingdom of God."

   d. Which of the fifteen "spiritual weeds" threatens your family and/or community the most?
   e. Which grows easier within you, the spiritual fruit or weeds? Why?

IV. To Work or Not To Work: (15 minutes)
   a. What does John 15:4–7 say is required for

changes to be made in the quantity and quality of spiritual fruit produced?

"Abide in me, and I in you. As the branch cannot bear fruit by itself, unless it abides in the vine, neither can you, unless you abide in me. I am the vine, you are the branches. He who abides in me, and I in him, he it is that bears much fruit, for apart from me you can do nothing. If a man does not abide in me, he is cast forth as a branch and withers; and the branches are gathered, thrown into the fire and burned. If you abide in me, and my words abide in you, ask whatever you will, and it shall be done for you."

b. Does "abiding in Christ" require any effort on our part?

c. *Four Corners*: Designate a different spiritual discipline (fasting, prayer, study, simplicity) for each corner of the room.

    i. Have participants choose the discipline in which they thrive, and have them go to that corner. There they will share the methods they find most helpful using that particular discipline.

    ii. *Then*, have the participants go to the corner that represents the spiritual discipline they struggle with the most, and have them share their struggles.

    iii.   Return to your seats, and share the "success stories."

V. What Must You Do? (10 minutes)

a. Based on your current calendar/day timer where can 10 minutes in your daily schedule be made for God to cultivate His fruit in you?

b. Read John 15:1–2 aloud:

> "I am the true vine, and my Father is the vinedresser. Every branch of mine that bears no fruit, He takes away, and every branch that does bear fruit He prunes, that it may bear more fruit."

c. If God is your spiritual gardener what might He cut off of your life right now so that you might grow more spiritual fruit?

d. Do you trust God to cut away things from your life?

e. Do you trust God to grow fruit in your life?

VI. The Story of Johnny Appleseed: (10 minutes)

a. What in Johnny Appleseed's life fulfilled what Jesus described in John 15:8?

> "By this my Father is glorified, that you bear much fruit, and so prove to be my disciples."

VII. Wrap Up: (2 minutes)
    a. Share prayer requests within the group.
    b. Confirm the time and location of the next group study.
    c. Close by reading out loud the following prayer:

Dear God,

Thanks for bringing us together to share in this fellowship and study. May all we do and say together honor and glorify You. Help us to open our hearts to whatever growth You would cultivate within us. We invite you to prune and fertilize us in whatever way we need, and may we do everything we can to cooperate with Your purposes. Inspire us to support one another's growth, honor each other's confidences, and encourage our mutual devotion to You and to one another. Bless us now as we part, trusting that you will bring us together again. Amen.

ENDNOTES

1 Dunnam, Maxie & Reisman, Kimberly, *The Workbook on Virtues and the Fruit of the Spirit*, Upper Room Books, Nashville. 1998 p. 124

2 USA Today, September 25th 2007

3 John Ortberg, *The life you've always wanted*, Zondervan, Grand Rapids, 1997. p. 72–73

4 *Brother Yun & Paul Hattaway, The Heavenly Man. London: Monarch Books*, 2002, 152–4

5 Oates, Stephen. *Let the Trumpet Sound*. New York: Harper Perennial. 1994 p. 87–89

6 Rev. Brian Bill, SermonCentral.com, Preparing For Patience

7 Rev. Brian Bill, SermonCentral.com, Preparing For Patience (Hope Health Letter 9/96).

8 Ibid.

9 Ibid.

10 Written by Jon Hinkson. He serves as a Senior Fellow at the Rivendell Institute for Thought and Learning in New Haven , CT.

11 Loftin, James. "Seize The Moment." Follow One International News Letter, Spring 2006

12 Teresa Neumann, "Boy's Sacrifice Takes Him to Yankee Stadium." Breaking Christian News@inJesus.com, (February 14th, 2006)

13 Davey, Monica, For Three Sons, It Was the Only Way: Turning Father In, the New York Times, December 29th, 2005.